Goose berry Patch Co. ™

A Country Store In Your Mailbox

Celebrate Summer

...sun-drenched days & starlit nights

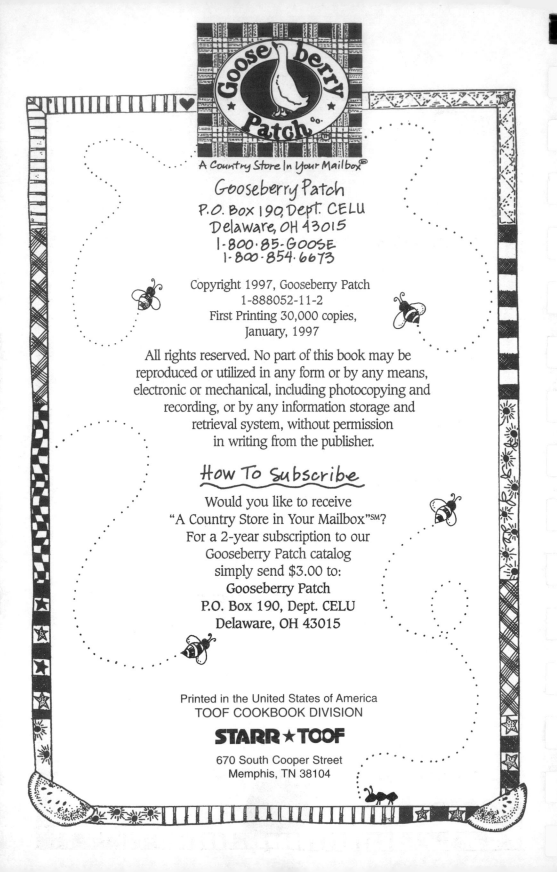

A Country Store In Your Mailbox®

Gooseberry Patch
P.O. Box 190, Dept. CELU
Delaware, OH 43015
1·800·85·GOOSE
1·800·854·6673

Copyright 1997, Gooseberry Patch
1-888052-11-2
First Printing 30,000 copies,
January, 1997

How To Subscribe

Would you like to receive
"A Country Store in Your Mailbox"℠?
For a 2-year subscription to our
Gooseberry Patch catalog
simply send $3.00 to:
Gooseberry Patch
P.O. Box 190, Dept. CELU
Delaware, OH 43015

Printed in the United States of America
TOOF COOKBOOK DIVISION

STARR★TOOF

670 South Cooper Street
Memphis, TN 38104

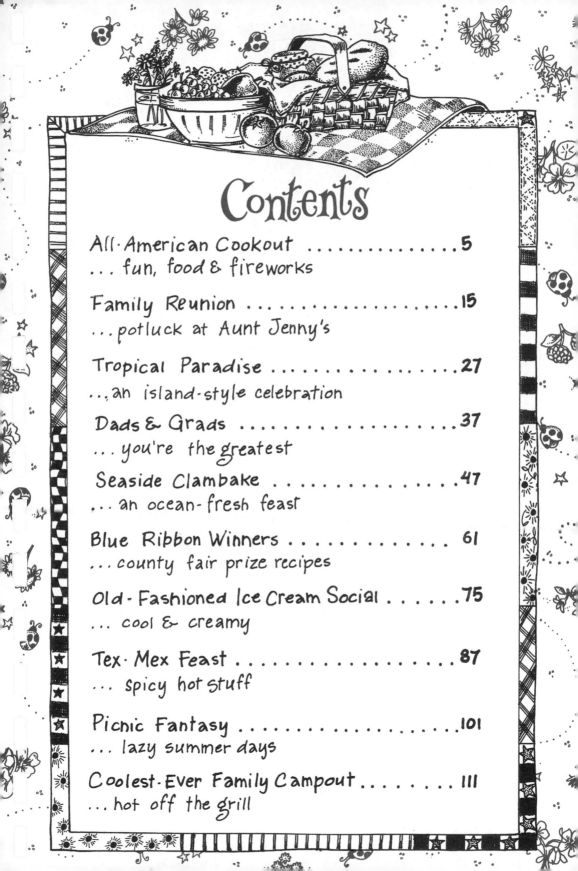

Contents

Dedication

To anyone who remembers the joy
of a golden summer day
and a red, ripe watermelon
under a big shade tree.

Appreciation

To all the friends of Gooseberry Patch
who generously share their
wishes, thoughts and laughter...
we thank you.

All-American Cookout

fun, food & fireworks

Grilled Garlic Burgers
Lime and Ginger Grilled Salmon
Creamed Peas
Grilled Vegetables
Summer Vegetable Salad
Blue Cheese Potato Salad
Minty Iced Tea
California Lemonade
Strawberry Shortcake

*Hats off! Along the street there comes
A blare of bugles, a ruffle of drums,
A flash of color beneath the sky:
Hats off!
The flag is passing by.*
- Henry Holcomb Bennett

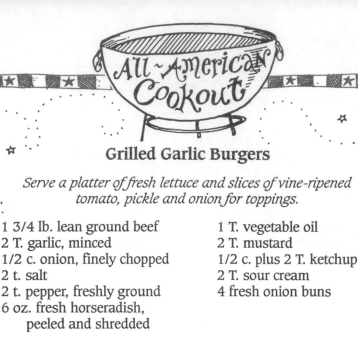

Grilled Garlic Burgers

Serve a platter of fresh lettuce and slices of vine-ripened tomato, pickle and onion for toppings.

1 3/4 lb. lean ground beef	1 T. vegetable oil
2 T. garlic, minced	2 T. mustard
1/2 c. onion, finely chopped	1/2 c. plus 2 T. ketchup
2 t. salt	2 T. sour cream
2 t. pepper, freshly ground	4 fresh onion buns
6 oz. fresh horseradish, peeled and shredded	

In a mixing bowl, mix ground beef, garlic, onion, salt and pepper. Shape into four patties. Sprinkle with horseradish and press into meat. Coat grill or large skillet with oil and cook burgers for 4 to 5 minutes per side. While cooking, mix together mustard, ketchup, and sour cream. Top with ketchup mixture and serve on grilled buns.

Turn the porch into a room that says "summer." Paint the floor white. If you have wicker or metal furniture, give it a fresh coat of white paint. Recover the cushions in fresh blue and white checks or stripes. Add a natural sisal mat or blue and white rag rug. If you have space, fill a windowbox with the colors of fresh plants in terra cotta pots...green ivies, yellow sunflowers, red geraniums.

Lime and Ginger Grilled Salmon

Arrange slices of fresh lemon and lime alongside.

2 lb. salmon fillet, skinned
    and boned
2 T. fresh ginger, minced
2 T. lime zest
1/2 t. salt

1/2 t. pepper, freshly ground
1/2 t. lime juice, freshly
    squeezed
2 T. butter, melted, or olive
    oil

Heat grill. Sprinkle salmon with ginger, lime zest, salt and pepper. In small bowl, combine lime juice and butter. Brush salmon with melted butter and grill about 5 minutes per side, or until done. Makes 4 servings.

Here's a foolproof method for grilling fish that'll keep it from falling apart and disappearing into the grill...make a "boat" out of a double thickness of aluminum foil. The boat will keep the fish moist and intact, yet still give it that unmistakable grilled flavor. Place the fish fillet (no more than 1-inch thick) in the center of the foil and fold over the edges, crimping to form a 1-inch edge all the way around the fish to catch drippings. Put seasonings over the fish and cook the fish, boat and all, uncovered on top of the grill for 8 to 10 minutes or until fish flakes easily with a fork. There's no need to turn the fish. To serve, top fish with some of the juices in the boat.

Creamed Peas

*Salmon and fresh peas are a traditional New England
Independence Day dish.*

1 T. sweet butter	4 c. peas, freshly shelled
1 T. vegetable oil	3 T. cream
1 c. onion, finely chopped	salt and pepper to taste

Melt butter in oil in a large saucepan over low heat. Add onion
and cook until tender and golden, about 15 minutes. Add peas
and just enough water to reach the top of the peas. Bring to a
simmer, cover and cook about 15 minutes, or until peas are very
tender. Add cream and cook until the liquid thickens into a
sauce, about 5 or 6 minutes. Season to taste.

*Spray paint a small brown paper bag bright red. Arrange little
flags in a glass or wide-mouthed jar and put inside the bag.
Fold the top of the bag down two or three times and tie with
a ribbon, raffia or strip of homespun. Makes a star-spangled
table decoration.*

Grilled Vegetables

Just a hint of charcoal gives veggies a delicious flavor.

summer squash, quartered
and seeded
zucchini, quartered and
seeded
onions, cut in half, unpeeled
yellow, red and green peppers,
halved and seeded

eggplant, quartered
mushrooms
tomatoes
scallions, trimmed

Marinade:

1 stick butter, melted
1/2 c. lemon juice, freshly
squeezed

1 T. fresh basil, chopped
pepper to taste

Melt butter and add lemon juice and seasonings. Coat all vegetables in the marinade. Skewer and cook on the grill, continuing to
baste while cooking. Note: onions, squash and eggplant take
longer to cook. Add peppers, mushrooms and tomatoes last.

*The second day of July, 1776...ought to be solemnized with pomp
and parade, with shows, games, sports, guns, bells, bonfires, and
illuminations, from one end of this continent to the other, from
this time forward forevermore.*
- John Adams, July 3, 1776 letter to Abigail Adams

All~American Cookout

Summer Vegetable Salad

A "just-right" medley of color, crunch and spice!

1 c. fresh asparagus,
   blanched and chopped
1 c. fresh tomatoes, seeded
   and chopped
1 c. zucchini, shredded
1 c. sweet red pepper, diced

2 t. balsamic vinegar
2 T. olive oil
7 dashes hot pepper sauce

Cook asparagus in small amount of boiling water until crisp-tender. In a salad bowl, combine tomatoes, zucchini, pepper and asparagus. In another bowl, whisk together vinegar, oil and hot pepper sauce. Combine dressing with salad just before serving.

*What is patriotism but the love of the good things
we ate in our childhood?*
- Lin Yutang

Blue Cheese Potato Salad

*Try a variation of this recipe with baby red potatoes...no need
to peel. Garnish with fresh dill.*

8 c. potatoes, boiled, peeled
   and cubed
1/2 c. scallions, chopped
1/2 c. celery, chopped
2 T. parsley, chopped
1/2 c. almond slivers, toasted
1/2 t. celery seed

2 t. salt
1/4 t. pepper, freshly ground
1/2 c. blue cheese, crumbled
2 c. sour cream
1/4 c. white wine vinegar

In a large bowl, combine potatoes, scallions, celery, parsley, almonds, celery seed, salt and pepper. In another bowl, mix together blue cheese, sour cream and vinegar. Pour over potatoes and toss to coat. Chill overnight.

Minty Iced Tea

For best tea results, always bring fresh, cold water to a rolling boil.

8 c. boiling water
8 mint herbal tea bags

8 c. ice cubes
fresh mint sprigs

In large glass container, pour water over tea bags and allow to steep for 30 minutes. Remove tea bags; stir in sugar to taste and half of ice cubes. Pour into glasses full of ice and top each with a fresh sprig of mint. Serves 12.

California Lemonade

Cardamom is a fragrant spice from India that tastes much like cinnamon.

1 1/2 c. sugar
1 c. lemon juice, freshly squeezed

5 cardamom seeds, ground

Boil sugar and lemon juice at medium heat for 8 to 10 minutes. Remove from heat and cool. Add cardamom seeds and store in refrigerator. To prepare lemonade, mix one tablespoon of concentrate with one cup sparkling water.

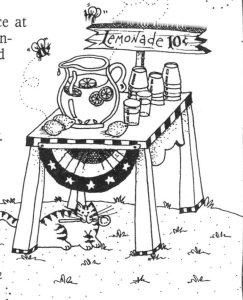

Strawberry Shortcake

For a luscious red, white and blue dessert, mix blueberries with your strawberries.

2 c. biscuit mix
2 T. sugar
1/2 c. milk
1/4 c. margarine, melted

1 qt. fresh ripe strawberries, hulled and sliced in two
fresh whipped cream

Preheat oven to 450 degrees. Beat biscuit mix, sugar, milk and margarine together until just mixed. Knead 8 to 10 times on lightly floured surface. Pat half of dough into an 8-inch round, greased pan. Bake for 15 to 20 minutes until golden. Let cool slightly, and remove from pan. Split shortcake crosswise and spoon strawberries in middle. Replace top half of shortcake and top with whipped cream.

Anchor the four corners of your picnic tablecloth with bricks. You can paint the bricks to match the occasion, using them over & over again. For a birthday party, tie the ribbons of helium balloons through the holes in the bricks. Instant celebration!

Red, white & beautiful...

Fabric Decorated Basket

Turn a plain wicker basket into a beautiful picnic basket!
You'll need:

a basket
spray paint
1/4 yard fabric with large
   printed design

1" wide paintbrush
clear acrylic spray
decoupage mix
soft cloth

Spray paint your basket and let dry completely. Cut out the design from your fabric and, following instructions on decoupage mix, brush onto wrong side of fabric. Place fabric over the basket and, using a warm, damp cloth, press the fabric in place around the body of the basket. Let dry. Spray basket with acrylic spray and let dry again. You might try an antique rose-colored fabric on a sage green basket, or cheery sunflowers on a hunter green basket. Line with a pretty kitchen towel and fill with goodies.

Sponge-Painted Napkins

Select a solid color cotton fabric for napkins. Cut fabric into 16-inch squares. Wash, dry and press with a warm iron. Sew a straight stitch all around the edges of the fabric, about 1/2-inch in from the edge. Fringe the fabric to the stitching. Trace the pattern you want on your napkins...stars, hearts, squares, diamonds...onto cardboard. Cut out the cardboard pattern and trace onto a sponge. Then cut out the sponge all around the pattern with an artist's blade. Dip the sponge in acrylic paint and stamp your pattern onto the napkin. After the paint has thoroughly dried, use a hot dry iron over a protective piece of cloth to set the paint.

Apple Candles

You'll need 12 or 13 apples and the same number of tea lights or votive candles, plus a lemon. Cut a thin slice off the bottom of each apple so it will stand upright. Core each apple, widening the space to accommodate a tea light or votive. Sprinkle lemon juice on the apple to keep it from turning brown. Insert your candles and light.

Luminaries

Light the way to your next evening celebration with a row of luminaries...beautiful on the beach or lighting a pathway to your late evening outdoor supper. Small brown lunch bags or white bakery bags work perfectly. Use a hole punch to create a design that will let the light shine through. Put sand, kitty litter or gravel in the bottoms of the bags to keep them firmly upright. Fill glass votives with candles and place in the bags, anchored by the sand. A charming glow!

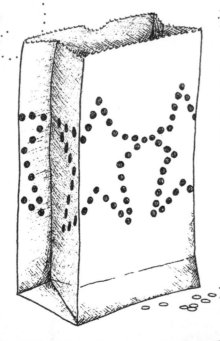

For a special effect, use heart or star-shaped hole punchers on your luminaries. If it's windy out, weigh the bags down by placing bricks inside.

Family Reunion

... potluck at Aunt Jenny's

Beer Steamed Shrimp
Barbecued Baby Back Ribs
Cornmeal Fried Chicken
Garlic Dill Pickles
Roasted Corn with Rosemary Butter
Mixed Green Slaw
Italian Cheesecake
Fudge Cake

*So it's home again, and home again, America for me.
My heart is turning home again, and there I long to be.*
- Henry Van Dyke

Family Reunion

Beer Steamed Shrimp

*Save your shrimp shells for up to three months
in the freezer...they can be boiled to make a
flavorful fish stock for chowder.*

2 T. lemon juice
1 T. prepared seafood seasoning

1 can beer
1 lb. shrimp, peeled
and deveined

In a large saucepan, combine lemon juice, seafood seasoning
and beer; bring to boil. Add shrimp; cover and steam for about 3
to 5 minutes until shrimp is pink and tender. Drain shrimp.
Serve hot or cold.

*Have a sign-up sheet at your reunion...get complete addresses,
phone numbers, names and ages of kids, occupations, etc. After
the reunion, type up the list and send it out to everyone
as a way of keeping in touch.*

Potluck at Aunt Jenny's

Barbecued Baby Back Ribs

Boiling the ribs first tenderizes them and removes excess fat.

2 T. olive oil
1 onion, chopped
1 stalk celery, chopped
1 clove garlic, peeled and
    finely chopped
1 c. ketchup

1/4 c. brown sugar, packed
1/4 c. red wine vinegar
2 T. Worcestershire sauce
1 T. Dijon mustard
1 1/2 lbs. baby back ribs

Heat oil in a saucepan, then add onion, celery and garlic. Sauté about 5 minutes, until tender. Add all remaining sauce ingredients, stirring and simmering for about 10 minutes. Put sauce in food processor and whirl until smooth. Allow sauce to cool slightly. Bring a pot of water to a boil; simmer ribs, covered, for about 20 minutes. Drain ribs and dry with paper towels; baste generously with sauce. Grill for 5 to 6 minutes on one side. Turn ribs and baste again. Grill for 6 minutes longer and serve with extra sauce.

*The heart that loves
is always young.*
- Greek proverb

Family Reunion

Cornmeal Fried Chicken

Orange flavor adds a sunny taste to this savory golden chicken!

3 T. orange zest
2 T. orange juice
1 c. milk
2/3 c. cornmeal
2/3 c. flour
1 t. salt

1 t. pepper, freshly ground
3 1/2 c. sunflower or
    safflower oil
3 lbs. frying chicken or 8
    chicken breasts

In a large bowl, combine orange zest, orange juice and milk. Soak chicken in this mixture for half an hour. Meanwhile, in a brown paper bag, combine cornmeal, flour, salt and pepper. Heat oil in a large skillet (filling about 2 inches deep) until it reaches 350 degrees. Coat chicken pieces one at a time by shaking in bag of cornmeal mixture. Fry chicken in oil about 20 minutes, or until juices run clear when pricked with a fork (breasts cook more quickly). Drain on paper towels.

A man travels the world over in search of what he needs
and returns home to find it.
    - George Moore

Potluck at Aunt Jenny's

Garlic Dill Pickles

2 1/2 qts. water
1/4 c. salt
2 T. vinegar
12 small cucumbers, rinsed
and trimmed

4 cloves garlic, peeled and
halved
4 t. fresh dill, coarsely chopped
2 chili peppers
1 t. pickling spice

Boil water, salt and vinegar. Pack cucumbers in two quart-size jars. Add hot water mixture, completely covering cucumbers. When cool, add garlic, dill, peppers and pickling spice. Cover lightly and let sit undisturbed for three days. Cover jar tightly and keep refrigerated.

Here's an idea for great fun at a family reunion...collect all the old family photos you can get your hands on. Label as best you can, and put albums together for all to enjoy.

Roasted Corn with Rosemary Butter

*What could be better than fresh sweet corn,
roasted in the husk?*

6 ears fresh corn, in husk
1/4 c. butter, softened

1 t. fresh rosemary
leaves, chopped

Pull back husks on corn, leaving them attached. Rinse corn and remove silk. Pat corn dry. In small bowl, mix together butter and rosemary; brush corn all over. Replace husks and roast corn on top of the grill for about 15 minutes, turning every so often until tender.

Have a "white elephant swap" at your family reunion. Ask everyone to bring something they'd like to get rid of...the more humorous the better. Have everyone take a number. Display all the "white elephants" on a table. At the end of the day, the person with #1 gets to choose his or her favorite item. The person with #2 has her choice, and so on until the "family heirlooms" are all gone.

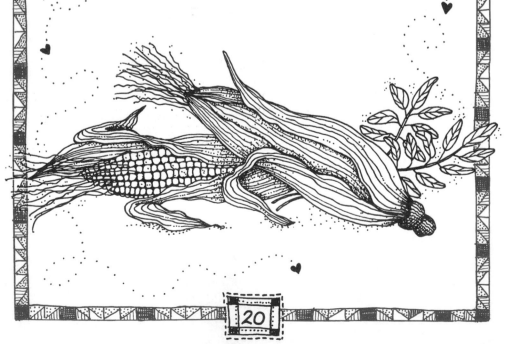

Mixed Green Slaw

A slaw without cabbage...cool, refreshing and low-fat.

2 c. romaine lettuce, thinly sliced
2 c. watercress, stems removed
2 c. radicchio, thinly sliced
1/2 c. plain low-fat yogurt

2 T. fresh lime juice
1 T. olive oil
salt and pepper to taste
1/4 c. green olives,
    pitted and chopped

Toss the greens together in a large salad bowl. In a separate bowl, whisk together the remaining ingredients. Toss the salad in the dressing just before serving. Serves 6.

Italian Cheesecake

*Easy to make, and it forms its own crust while baking! Top
with fresh berries of your choice.*

2-8 oz. pkgs. cream
    cheese
1 lb. ricotta cheese
1 pt. sour cream
1 1/2 c. sugar

4 eggs
5 t. vanilla extract
5 t. lemon juice
3 t. flour
3 t. cornstarch

Beat the cream cheese, ricotta cheese and sour cream together. Add sugar and continue to beat. Add all remaining ingredients, one at a time, beating well until mixture is very well combined. Pour the batter into a greased 9-inch springform pan and bake at 350 degrees for one hour. Turn off the oven and, keeping the door closed, leave the cake in the oven for one hour longer. Remove cake and allow to cool on rack, then put in the refrigerator overnight. Remove sides of the pan, and keep chilled until ready to serve.

*Be sure to appoint one person as the "official photographer" at
your reunion, and send reprints of special photos to family
members.*

Family Reunion

Fudge Cake

Feel free to indulge...this delicious recipe is fat-free!

1 c. flour
1/3 c. plus 1 T. unsweetened
  cocoa powder
1 t. instant coffee powder
1 t. baking powder
1 t. baking soda
6 large egg whites, room
  temperature

1 1/3 c. light brown sugar,
  firmly packed
1 c. coffee-flavored fat-free
  yogurt
1 t. vanilla extract
1 t. powdered sugar
1/2 t. ground cinnamon

Line the bottom of a 9-inch cake pan with waxed paper; spray pan and paper with vegetable oil spray. Dust with flour. Sift flour, 1/3 cup cocoa, coffee powder, baking powder and soda into a medium bowl. In a separate bowl, beat egg whites, brown sugar, yogurt and vanilla about 2 minutes. Combine with dry ingredients. Pour batter into cake pan and bake in a preheated 350 degree oven about 35 minutes, or until toothpick comes out clean. Cool in pan for 10 minutes, then loosen cake and turn out onto cake plate. Peel off paper. Mix together powdered sugar, tablespoon of cocoa powder and cinnamon. Sift over the top of the cake when it is completely cool.

Relatively speaking...

Recipe Cards and Holder

A family reunion is a great time to catch up, have fun, and enjoy family cooking! Someone is going to ask for a favorite recipe...it always happens...so this time, be prepared. Make some recipe cards and holders for each family. They're quick, easy, and sure to be a hit. You'll need:

scraps of coordinating fabrics
giant clothespins
craft glue
marking pen

tracing paper
pinking shears
3"x5" index cards

You can find big, 7-inch clothespins at most craft stores. Make a patterns of two hearts, one smaller than the other. Trace the heart patterns onto the tracing paper and cut out. Place heart patterns on fabric and draw around outline. Cut hearts out of fabric with pinking shears. Cut out three 3-inch hearts for each recipe holder, and as many smaller hearts as you wish to decorate the recipe cards. Glue large hearts vertically onto the clothespin, overlapping them one above the other. Glue a small heart onto the back of each index card. Tie a bundle of recipe cards together with jute and clip with the clothespin to give to relatives. Note: You can use this idea with other designs... for instance, you might want to use the initial of your family name instead of a heart pattern.

Heirloom Photo Button Jar

This makes a special gift for a family member. Make a number of them to distribute, or use as door prizes.

canning jar with lid
photocopy of old photograph
glossy wood-tone spray

3/4"W lace
1/4"W satin ribbon
craft glue

Spray your photocopy lightly with wood-tone spray and let dry. When dry, use the jar lid as a pattern to cut around the photocopy. Apply craft glue lightly to the top of the jar lid, then glue photo to the lid and top with the screw ring. Fill jar with old buttons, potpourri, marbles, dry beans or anything you'd like! Place the lid on the jar and glue lace around the screw ring. Tie ribbon on top of lace.

Family Tree

A family reunion is the perfect time to display your family tree. If you've saved photographs through the years, you may be able to put one together for your family.

18" lengths of thick paper-
    covered wire for branches
photocopies of family photos
6" square of 1-1/2" thick green
    florist's foam

sheet moss
narrow ribbon or cord
craft glue

Use the paper-covered wire to make the branches. The number of branches you'll need on your tree depends on how many family members there are. Once the branches are counted, double the number so you can twist two pieces of wire together for each branch. For example, if you have 4 children and 10 grandchildren, you would have 14 descendants and would need 28 pieces of paper-covered wire. Begin by grouping all the pieces of wire together. Two inches from the bottom, twist the wire together until it forms a 6-inch trunk. Spread out the 2-inch bottom pieces...these will form the "roots" of the tree. At the top of your tree, divide the branches into groups of families, depending on how many people are in each family. Twist each group of wires together to make branches, leaving the strands fanned out at the ends to hold your pictures. Using the florist's foam as a base, cover it with sheet moss. Place the roots of your tree into the foam for support. Punch a hole at the top of each photo. Attach a loop of ribbon or cord to each photo and tie to branches of the tree by family grouping.

Family Photo Calendar

Using a wall calendar, select twelve family photos. If you have photos of festive occasions such as anniversaries, birthdays and weddings, these will work very well. Make a color photocopy of each photo, enlarged to the size of the calendar page. Carefully glue one onto each month. A great gift!

♥ Photo Puzzle

Take any favorite family picture...of a wedding, reunion, graduation, or any occasion...and turn it into a puzzle. Have the photo enlarged and mount it on a piece of foam board with spray glue. Cover the picture with tracing paper and draw a puzzle pattern onto the paper. Using a sharp utility knife, carefully cut through the tracing paper, photo and foam board along your puzzle pattern lines. Gently separate the pieces and your family puzzle is ready!

Grandparent's Brag Book

Make a scrapbook just for grandparents, who love to show off their grandchildren's latest accomplishments. Fill it with photos, awards, hand-drawn pictures and a personal note from the grandchild. It's easy...use a small photo album with lots of pages. Tuck in all of your special items and you have an instant brag book. Let the grandchildren decorate the cover with pictures of their artwork.

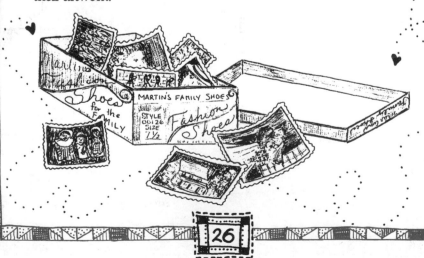

Tropical Paradise

...an island-style celebration

Coconut Shrimp
Ham & Pineapple Kabobs
Chicken Salad with Melon
Teriyaki Steak Strips
Tomato Frittata
Ginger Coconut Tart
Piña Colada Pie
Bananas Rum Flambé

*If there is a paradise on
the face of the earth,
It is this, oh! It is this!*
- Indian inscription

Coconut Shrimp

Garnish with fresh orange slices.

1 1/2 c. oil
1 c. flour
1 c. beer

14 oz. pkg. shredded coconut
1 lb. shrimp, shelled and
   cleaned

Pour oil into large fryer and heat to 375 degrees. Mix together flour and beer until it makes a batter. Coat shrimp in batter, then roll in coconut. Fry shrimp in small batches about 2 to 3 minutes until golden and curled. Drain on paper towels.

How to cook shrimp on the beach: First, build a fire. Bring a large pot of water to boil. Throw in a few lemon halves and some garlic. Cook in the shell until they turn pinkish-white (depending on size of the shrimp, 5-10 minutes). Peel and eat.

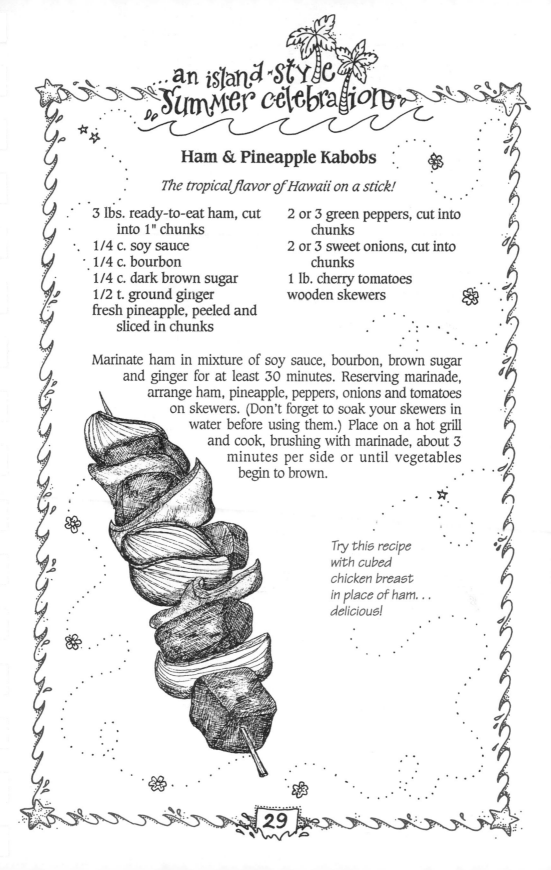

...an island-style Summer celebration

Ham & Pineapple Kabobs

The tropical flavor of Hawaii on a stick!

3 lbs. ready-to-eat ham, cut into 1" chunks
1/4 c. soy sauce
1/4 c. bourbon
1/4 c. dark brown sugar
1/2 t. ground ginger
fresh pineapple, peeled and sliced in chunks

2 or 3 green peppers, cut into chunks
2 or 3 sweet onions, cut into chunks
1 lb. cherry tomatoes
wooden skewers

Marinate ham in mixture of soy sauce, bourbon, brown sugar and ginger for at least 30 minutes. Reserving marinade, arrange ham, pineapple, peppers, onions and tomatoes on skewers. (Don't forget to soak your skewers in water before using them.) Place on a hot grill and cook, brushing with marinade, about 3 minutes per side or until vegetables begin to brown.

Try this recipe with cubed chicken breast in place of ham. . . delicious!

Chicken Salad with Melon

Be sure to make enough to pack your lunch the next day!

1 envelope chicken bouillon
4 skinless, boneless chicken
   breasts
2 T. honey
1/2 c. sour cream
1 T. Dijon mustard
salt and pepper to taste
1/2 c. scallions, chopped

1 medium cantaloupe,
   seeded and balled
1/2 medium honeydew
   melon, seeded and balled
1 medium papaya, seeded
   and sliced into 1/4" slices
8 leaves fresh leaf lettuce

To prepare chicken, bring bouillon and 2" water to boil in 2-quart saucepan. Reduce heat and add chicken breasts; simmer covered for 20 minutes. Meanwhile prepare dressing by whisking together honey, sour cream, mustard, salt and pepper. Stir in scallions and set aside. After chicken has simmered, cool and cut into cubes; mix with cantaloupe and honeydew. Pour dressing over chicken-melon mixture and toss to coat thoroughly. To serve, arrange lettuce leaves and papaya slices on plates and place scoops of chicken salad in the center.

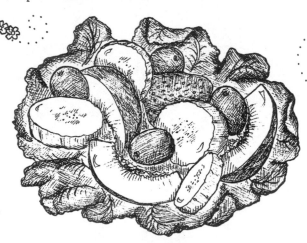

Friends are like melons. Shall I tell you why?
To find one good, you must a hundred try.
- Claude Mermet

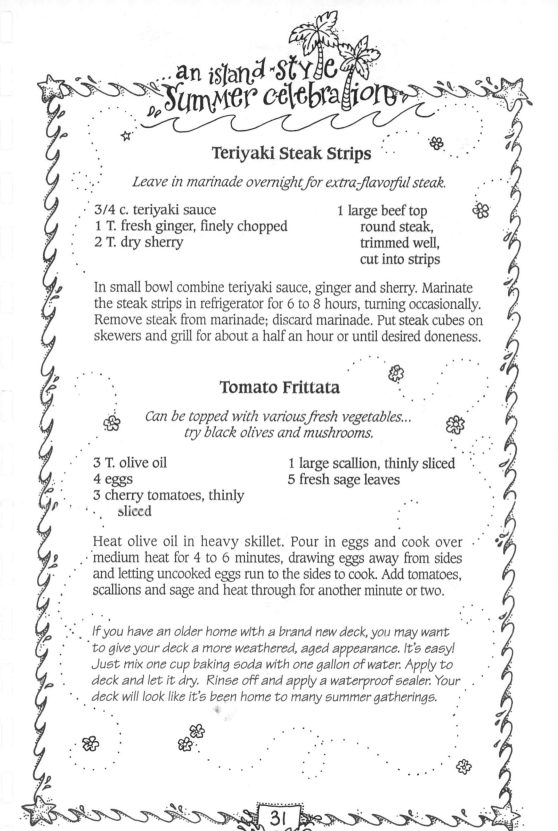

Teriyaki Steak Strips

Leave in marinade overnight for extra-flavorful steak.

3/4 c. teriyaki sauce
1 T. fresh ginger, finely chopped
2 T. dry sherry

1 large beef top
   round steak,
   trimmed well,
   cut into strips

In small bowl combine teriyaki sauce, ginger and sherry. Marinate the steak strips in refrigerator for 6 to 8 hours, turning occasionally. Remove steak from marinade; discard marinade. Put steak cubes on skewers and grill for about a half an hour or until desired doneness.

Tomato Frittata

Can be topped with various fresh vegetables...
try black olives and mushrooms.

3 T. olive oil
4 eggs
3 cherry tomatoes, thinly
   sliced

1 large scallion, thinly sliced
5 fresh sage leaves

Heat olive oil in heavy skillet. Pour in eggs and cook over medium heat for 4 to 6 minutes, drawing eggs away from sides and letting uncooked eggs run to the sides to cook. Add tomatoes, scallions and sage and heat through for another minute or two.

If you have an older home with a brand new deck, you may want to give your deck a more weathered, aged appearance. It's easy! Just mix one cup baking soda with one gallon of water. Apply to deck and let it dry. Rinse off and apply a waterproof sealer. Your deck will look like it's been home to many summer gatherings.

Ginger Coconut Tart

*Buy the shredded coconut already prepared. You may
substitute fresh, ripe sliced pears
if papayas aren't available. Delicious!*

1 prepared pie crust, baked
8 oz. pkg. cream cheese,
  room temperature
6 T. cream of coconut
  (canned)
3 T. sugar

1 c. sweetened shredded
  coconut, toasted
1/4 c. crystallized ginger,
  chopped
2 large papayas, peeled and
  thinly sliced
1/2 c. apricot preserves

Bake pie crust according to package directions (or make your
own favorite pie crust and bake 'til golden brown). Beat cream
cheese with a mixer until smooth, then add cream of coconut,
sugar, 3/4 cup of the toasted coconut and the ginger. Spread
filling in pie crust. Place papaya slices in attractive
arrangement on top of filling. In a small
saucepan, heat preserves over low heat,
stirring until melted. Brush preserves
over the top of the tart. Sprinkle
remaining coconut over the
top. Refrigerate at least 1
hour, or until firm.

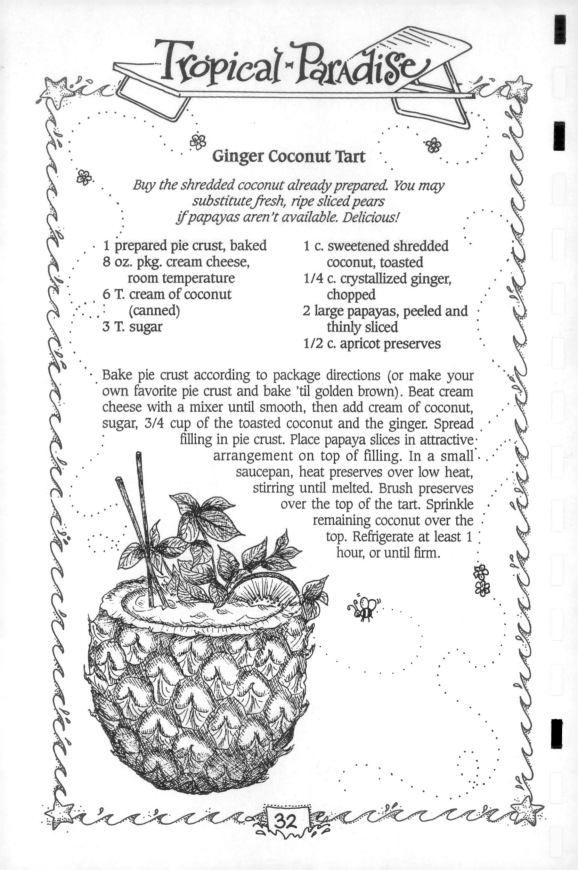

Piña Colada Pie

Prepare this delicious tropical pie ahead of time and pull it out of the freezer like magic!

Crust:

1/2 lb. mixed nuts, shelled and finely chopped
3/4 c. sweetened shredded coconut, chopped

3 T. brown sugar
1 T. sweet butter, melted

Filling:

1 1/2 pt. pineapple sorbet, softened
3/4 c. canned cream of coconut
3 T. dark rum

1/2 t. coconut extract
3/4 c. sweetened shredded coconut
1 qt. vanilla ice cream, softened

Garnish:

1/2 pineapple, peeled and thinly sliced
1/4 c. sweetened shredded coconut, toasted

fresh mint sprigs

Line a 10-inch glass pie plate with foil, overlapping the sides. Mix nuts, coconut, brown sugar and butter until crumbs are formed. Press crumbs firmly onto bottom and sides of pie dish. Freeze 10 minutes, then bake in a 350 degree oven about 15 minutes, until golden brown. When crust has cooled, freeze another 20 minutes. Spread pineapple sorbet smoothly over crust and place in the freezer. In a small saucepan, bring cream of coconut to a boil, stirring frequently, for about 3 minutes. Pour into a bowl and add rum, coconut extract and shredded coconut. Allow to cool, then fold in vanilla ice cream until blended. Freeze this filling mixture, stirring occasionally, about 1 hour. Spoon ice cream filling over sorbet layer in pie dish, making a nice mounded shape. Cover and freeze overnight. Turn pie upside down onto a platter and remove foil. Turn pie right side up. Garnish with pineapple, coconut and mint.

Bananas Rum Flambé

A dramatic ending to a perfect tropical evening.

1/4 c. orange juice
   concentrate
1 1/2 T. lemon juice
2 T. butter
1/3 c. brown sugar, packed

2 bananas, peeled and sliced
   diagonally
1/4 c. rum
1 qt. vanilla ice cream

In a large skillet, heat orange juice concentrate, lemon juice, butter and sugar until bubbling. Add bananas. In a small saucepan, warm the rum, remove from heat, then carefully ignite with a long kitchen match. Remove bananas and sauce from heat and carefully pour rum over it while still in the skillet. Pour bananas and sauce over individual servings of ice cream. Serves 6.

Once bananas are sliced, sprinkle with lemon juice to keep them from turning brown.

Summer Party Pointers...

Lighting Ideas

Lighting is extremely important to the atmosphere of any party. Most parties need two types of lighting...one to light the scenery and the other to add glow to tables and other eating areas. You can achieve a party mood with bamboo torches, paper lanterns, luminarias (votive candles nestled in sand inside open paper bags), strings of colored lights or tiny white lights. For table lighting, use votive candles tucked inside colored beverage glasses, jelly jars or little clay pots. Taper candles work well inside hurricane shades, and pillar candles can be placed inside crocks, buckets and big clay pots. For even more sparkle, string tiny white lights along your buffet table.

Float fresh gardenias and candles in water in a shallow clear glass bowl for a tropical centerpiece.

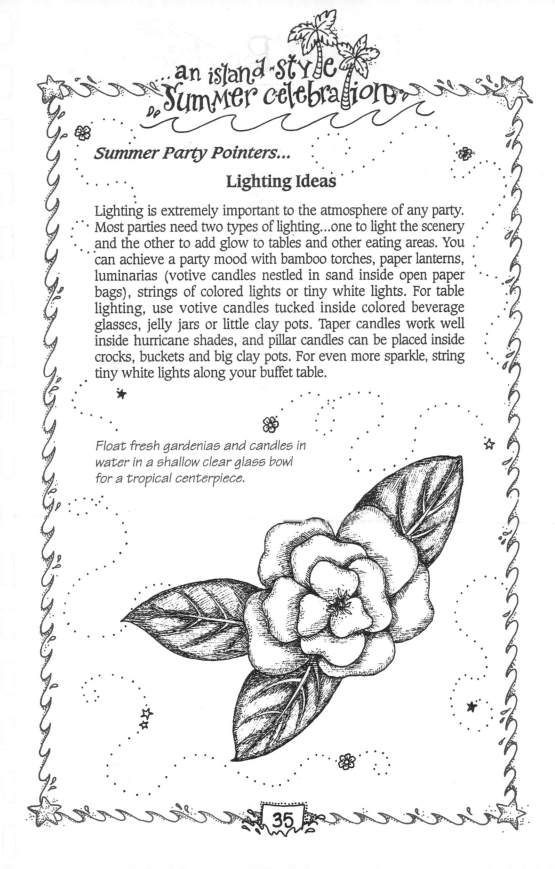

Tropical-Paradise

Fresh Fruit Ices

Make a variety of cool, refreshing fruit ices with just a few ingredients:

1 envelope unflavored
   gelatin
1/2 c. cold water
1 c. juice of your choice...
   orange, grapefruit,
   cranberry, strawberry,
   apple, cherry
6 T. freshly-squeezed lemon
   juice

4 T. sugar
1 c. sliced strawberries,
   peaches or melon
3 bananas, mashed
lemon or lime slice
superfine sugar
citrus slices as garnish

Soften gelatin in the water. Place in a saucepan over low heat and stir until gelatin is completely dissolved. Add juices, sugar and fruit and stir. Pour into a bowl and put in the freezer until almost set. With an electric mixer, beat on highest speed until light and fluffy. Cover and return to freezer to set. For an extra treat, chill glasses in the freezer. When ready to serve, run a slice of lemon or lime around the rims of glasses, turn upside down and dip in superfine sugar, then fill with fruit ice. Garnish with a slice of orange, lemon or lime. Serves 8.

Lemon-Scented Towels

Any party menu that includes finger foods will call for extra clean-up. Pamper your guests with warm, lemon-scented towels. Soak little fingertip towels in a mixture of water and lemon juice. Fold and roll them up, then microwave for 10 to 15 seconds. Serve them up on a tray just before dessert. Very luxurious!

Dads & Grads

...you're the greatest!

Chunky Gazpacho
Ginger-Lime Salad
Grilled Strip Steaks with Herb Mustard Sauce
Pan-Fried Trout
Buttery Roasted Potatoes
Fresh Corn Cakes
Blackberry-Apple Crunch

Life is a song - sing it.
Life is a game - play it.
Life is a challenge - meet it.
Life is a dream - realize it.
Life is a sacrifice - offer it.
Life is love - enjoy it.
- Sai Baba

Chunky Gazpacho

Fresh tomatoes from the garden make this gazpacho very special. Serve in big, icy mugs garnished with stalks of celery.

2 1/2 c. tomato juice
3 T. lemon juice
1/4 c. plus 1 T. olive oil
6 large tomatoes, peeled and
    chopped
2 cucumbers, peeled, seeded
    and chopped

1/2 c. green peppers, seeded
    and chopped
1/2 c. onion, finely chopped
1 clove garlic, minced
hot pepper sauce to taste
salt and pepper to taste

Whisk together tomato juice, lemon juice and olive oil; set aside. In large mixing bowl, combine the chopped vegetables; pour dressing over vegetables and mix. Add hot pepper sauce, salt and pepper to taste. Cover and chill. Serve cold.

Ginger-Lime Salad

The surprising taste of peaches makes this a very refreshing salad.

1 head green leaf lettuce, torn
1 ripe peach, pitted and thinly sliced

2 T. fresh parsley, torn

Dressing:

1 1/2 T. fresh ginger, grated
3 T. lime juice
salt and pepper to taste

6 T. olive oil
1 1/2 t. honey

In a large salad bowl, toss together lettuce, peaches and parsley. In small mixing bowl, whisk dressing ingredients together and pour over lettuce. Season to taste with salt and pepper and serve chilled.

Grilled Strip Steaks with Herb Mustard Sauce

Who can resist the aroma of steaks on the grill?

Herb Mustard Sauce:

2 cloves garlic, crushed
2 t. water
2 T. Dijon mustard

1 t. basil
1/2 t. pepper
1/2 t. thyme

2 boneless strip or ribeye steaks, 2-1/2 to 3" thick
salt to taste

On high power, microwave garlic and water together. Stir in mustard, basil, pepper and thyme; spread onto both sides of steaks. Place steaks on grid over medium ash-covered coals and grill. Grill loin steaks 8 or 9 minutes per side, ribeye steaks 6 to 7 minutes per side (depending on thickness) for medium-rare to medium doneness. Season steaks with salt as desired. Carve steaks crosswise into thick slices. Makes 4 servings.

To have grown wise and kind is the greatest success of all.
-Anonymous

Pan-Fried Trout

If your celebration includes a fishing trip, fresh trout is the way to go!

1/2 c. cornmeal
1/2 c. flour
3/4 T. salt
1 T. pepper

2 onions, thinly sliced
1 lb. bacon, fried (reserve some of grease)
1 or 2 fresh trout, cleaned

Mix together corn meal, flour, salt and pepper; set aside. In large frying pan, sauté onions in bacon grease. Dredge fish in corn-meal mixture and coat both sides well. Fry fish in hot grease and onions until very crisp. Garnish with crispy bacon.

Life isn't a matter of milestones,
but of moments.
-Rose Fitzgerald Kennedy

You're the Greatest!

Buttery Roasted Potatoes

If you have a large cast-iron skillet, it's the very best pan for roasting your potatoes.

2 lbs. Yukon Gold potatoes,   hot water
  peeled and cut into 1"   2 t. salt
  cubes

Preheat oven to 400 degrees. Place potatoes in a large cast-iron skillet and pour in enough hot water to cover about 1/4 inch of the potatoes. Scatter bits of butter over potatoes and season; then stir. Bake uncovered about 60 minutes, until potatoes are lightly browned and water has evaporated.

Real joy comes not from ease or riches or from the praise of men, but from doing something worthwhile.
- Sir Wilfred Grenfell

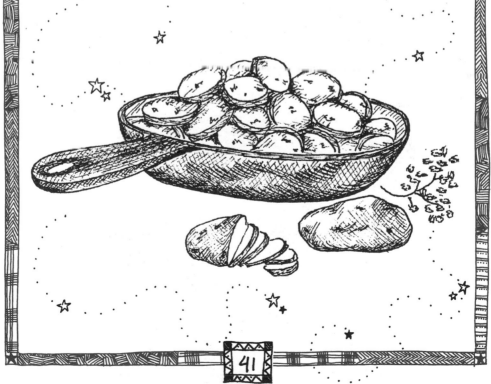

Fresh Corn Cakes

Fresh sweet corn is the very taste of summer.

4 ears yellow or white sweet
   corn, husked
1/2 c. cornmeal
1/2 c. flour
1 t. salt
1 t. sugar
1/2 t. baking powder

1/4 t. cayenne pepper
1 large egg, beaten
3/4 c. buttermilk
3 T. sweet butter, melted
2 scallions, finely chopped
1 c. sour cream with chives

Cook corn in boiling water for one minute and drain. Cut kernels from the cobs and mash lightly. In a small bowl, combine cornmeal, flour, salt, sugar, baking powder and pepper. In a separate bowl, whisk egg, buttermilk and butter. Add egg mixture to dry ingredients and stir lightly. Stir in scallions and corn. In a heated, well-seasoned iron skillet that has been coated with oil, place heaping tablespoons of the batter; brown and flip as you would pancakes. Serve sour cream alongside.

The best and most beautiful things in the world
cannot be seen nor touched...but are felt in the heart.
- Helen Keller

You're the Greatest!

Blackberry-Apple Crunch

This dish tastes delicious after a day of blackberry-picking!

2 1/4 c. flour
2 1/2 c. sugar
1/4 t. salt
1 c. butter, sliced
2 1/2 c. fresh blackberries

4 lbs. Golden Delicious
apples, peeled, cored and
thinly sliced
sprinkle of cinnamon

Preheat oven to 350 degrees. Grease a 13"x9" baking dish. In medium mixing bowl, combine 2 cups flour, 1 1/2 cups sugar and salt. Cut in butter with pastry blender and mix until crumbly. In another bowl, toss together blackberries, apples, remaining flour and remaining sugar; pour into baking dish. Cover with crumbly topping, sprinkle with cinnamon and bake for about 15 minutes until fruit bubbles. Cool slightly and serve.

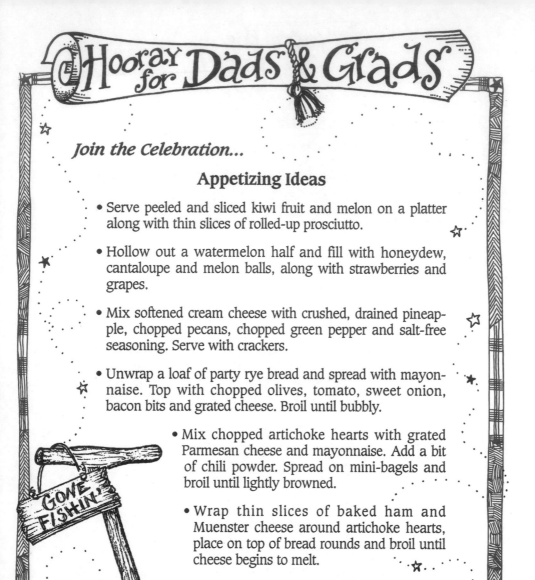

Hooray for Dads & Grads

Join the Celebration...

Appetizing Ideas

- Serve peeled and sliced kiwi fruit and melon on a platter along with thin slices of rolled-up prosciutto.

- Hollow out a watermelon half and fill with honeydew, cantaloupe and melon balls, along with strawberries and grapes.

- Mix softened cream cheese with crushed, drained pineapple, chopped pecans, chopped green pepper and salt-free seasoning. Serve with crackers.

- Unwrap a loaf of party rye bread and spread with mayonnaise. Top with chopped olives, tomato, sweet onion, bacon bits and grated cheese. Broil until bubbly.

- Mix chopped artichoke hearts with grated Parmesan cheese and mayonnaise. Add a bit of chili powder. Spread on mini-bagels and broil until lightly browned.

- Wrap thin slices of baked ham and Muenster cheese around artichoke hearts, place on top of bread rounds and broil until cheese begins to melt.

- Unwrap an 8-ounce block of cream cheese and pour salsa over the top. Serve with crackers.

GONE FISHIN'

Father's Day Memory Box

Presented on Father's Day, this reminder of the past will be a welcome gift.

wooden box
acrylic paint
wood-tone spray finish
craft glue
photocopies of old photographs

decoupage sealer
walnut water-based stain
fine-grain sandpaper
paintbrushes
photo mounting corners

Paint your box (we used burgundy for a rich color). While it's drying, lightly spray your photocopies with the wood-tone spray. Set them aside to dry, also. When the photocopies are dry, glue photo mounting corners to some of the photocopies. Arrange your photos on the box lid in any position you like. Use sealer to glue the photos to the box lid and allow to dry thoroughly. When photocopies are dry, apply the walnut sealer to the entire box, removing any excess with a soft cloth. Allow to dry according to directions. Once dry, apply five coats of sealer to the box, allowing each coat to dry before applying the next.

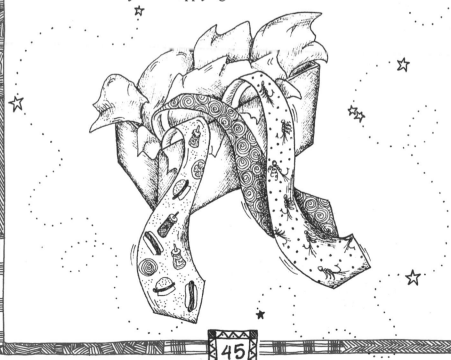

Graduation Cap Gift Box

Choose school colors for the ribbon. A very unique gift to fill with money, candy, childhood photos or homemade cookies.

8" round wooden cheese box
tacky glue
craft brush
5/8 yard satin ribbon

10" square mat board
14" square of fabric
tassel (from fabric
   store)
hot glue gun

Using a craft brush, apply glue to the outer rim on the upper lid of the box. Attach ribbon to the rim. Brush one side of the mat board with glue and place on the wrong side of your fabric. Fold each side of the fabric in, smoothing out any bumps, and let dry thoroughly. Put a small hole in the middle of the board and pull the tassel cord through from the top using hot glue to attach it to the underside. Fasten the underside of the board to the top of the box lid with hot glue. Center the square on top of the circle to represent a graduation cap.

"Good Luck" Boxes

If you're sending a high school grad off to college, here's a thoughtful way to say, "We're thinking of you." Gather old photos of family members and friends sharing good times together. Collect special mementos...old programs, ticket stubs, newspaper clippings. Select your grad's favorite snack, magazines, stationery and stamps. Put everything in a box. Obtain a map of the grad's destination and use the map to wrap the box.

Seaside Clambake

... an ocean-fresh feast

Steamers
New England Clam Chowder
Red Pepper Shrimp
Grilled Jumbo Shrimp
Spicy Cocktail Sauce
Oysters Rockefeller
Crab-Potato Cakes
Cornmeal Biscuits
Blueberry Lemon Mousse
Lemon Crunch Cookies

The sea! the sea! the open sea!
The blue, the fresh, the ever free.
— Barry Cornwall

Seaside Clambake

Steamers

"Steamers" is another word for littleneck clams. A bucket of steamers served with ice cold beer is an East Coast tradition. Here's an easy microwave version in a delicious light sauce.

2 dozen littleneck clams, well-scrubbed
1 T. salt
1 T. cornmeal
1/2 c. dry white wine
1/2 c. water

4 T. sweet butter
2 shallots, peeled and chopped
2 T. fresh parsley, chopped
2 cloves garlic, minced
ripe red tomato, diced

Cover clams with cold water in a large bowl. Sprinkle with salt and cornmeal. Let stand for about an hour. Rinse and drain. Put all other ingredients in a large microwave-safe casserole dish and stir. Cook on high, uncovered, 5 minutes. Add clams, cover and cook 5 or 6 minutes, or until clams open. Serves 4.

New England Clam Chowder

2 T. flour
1 c. milk
2-8 oz. bottles clam juice

2-10 oz. cans baby clams in juice
1 lb. new potatoes, boiled and cubed

Dissolve the flour in the milk and set aside. In a medium saucepan, combine the clam juice, clams, and potatoes. Simmer over medium-high heat. Gradually add the milk mixture, stirring constantly, and bring to a boil. Stir for about 3 minutes until soup thickens. Serve immediately.

Fill empty clamshells with melted wax and stick votive candles in the middle for a glowy beach atmosphere.

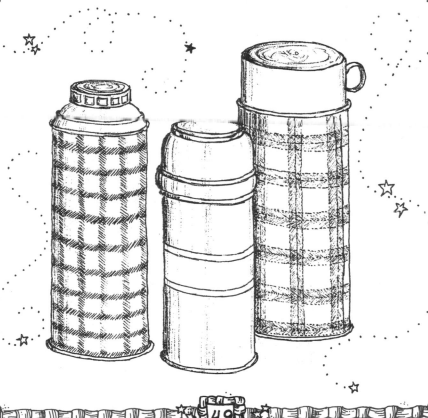

Seaside Clambake

Red Pepper Shrimp

Delicious on a bed of soft, brown rice.

1/4 c. olive oil
1/2 t. dried hot pepper flakes
1 1/2 lbs. shrimp, shelled and cleaned

1/2 t. salt
1/3 c. dry white wine

Combine olive oil and hot pepper flakes. Add shrimp and stir to coat. Marinate for 5 to 10 minutes. Heat a heavy frying pan and add shrimp and oil. Cook shrimp over medium-high heat until shrimp are golden pink, about 2 minutes on each side. Remove shrimp and place in serving bowl. Pour salt and wine into frying pan and bring to a boil. Pour over the shrimp and serve right away.

You can make an easy vegetable-kabob with tender baby veggies. Try zucchini, pattypan, baby yellow and sunburst squash, baby carrots, cherry tomatoes and pearl onions. Brush with olive oil, season and grill.

Grilled Jumbo Shrimp ☆

Alternate the shrimp with ripe cherry tomatoes on the skewer.

2 lbs. jumbo shrimp, peeled and deveined

Marinade: ★

1/4 c. soy sauce
1 c. orange juice
1/4 c. olive oil
4 T. sugar

3 garlic cloves, minced
1 T. fresh ginger, finely
    chopped
1 T. lemon zest

In a small bowl, whisk together marinade ingredients. Add shrimp and marinate in refrigerator for at least one hour, stirring occasionally. Thread shrimp onto skewers and barbecue about 2 minutes on each side, basting occasionally with marinade. Serves 6.

*The gods do not deduct from man's allotted
span the hours spent in fishing.*
- Babylonian proverb

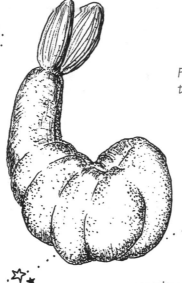

*For easier munching, leave
the tail on the shrimp.*

Spicy Cocktail Sauce

Sauce can be prepared and refrigerated for up to 2 weeks.

8 to 10 plum tomatoes, peeled, seeded and chopped
6 cloves garlic, minced
1 stalk celery, finely chopped
1 medium onion, finely chopped
1/4 t. cayenne pepper
1/2 t. salt

2 T. sugar
2 T. lemon juice
3 T. tomato paste
1 T. Worcestershire sauce
1/3 c. red wine vinegar
2 T. balsamic vinegar
1 T. horseradish, finely chopped

Combine all ingredients except for horseradish in medium saucepan. Cover and simmer on low heat for 30 to 40 minutes, stirring every 10 minutes. Stir in horseradish. Refrigerate for at least 30 minutes, allowing flavors to blend. Makes 2 1/4 cups.

Make your home summery with fresh cotton sheets in ice-cream colors. Hang them in the windows with café clips or spring-rods, tying back with wide, soft ribbons. Use sheets to cover tables on porches and patios; spread them on the beds in place of heavy comforters.

Oysters Rockefeller

A New Orleans restaurant first created this dish in the late 1800's. Though the original recipe had no spinach, we've included it in ours because it adds delicious flavor.

4 T. sweet butter, room temperature
1/4 c. dried bread crumbs
1 T. green onions, sliced
1/4 c. spinach, finely chopped
1/4 c. celery, finely chopped

1 T. fresh tarragon leaves, chopped
1/4 t. salt
freshly ground pepper to taste
cayenne pepper to taste
12 fresh oysters on the half shell

Combine butter, bread crumbs, onion, spinach, celery, tarragon and seasonings and pureé in a food processor until smooth. With a small, sharp knife, cut underneath each oyster to loosen it from its shell. Arrange oysters in their shells on a baking sheet. Spread pureéd mixture over each oyster. Broil under a preheated broiler 2 to 3 minutes, just until crisp and golden. Serve immediately. Serves 2 to 4.

Surround a pillar candle with seashells for a pretty table decoration.

Seaside Clambake

Crab-Potato Cakes

Garnish these cakes with fresh, red tomato slices and basil leaves.

2 T. mayonnaise
1/8 t. hot pepper sauce
2 egg whites, lightly beaten
1/4 t. dry mustard
3/4 t. lemon zest, grated
1 1/2 t. fresh lemon juice
1/8 t. salt
2 t. celery, finely chopped

3 T. parsley, minced
1 T. green onions, finely chopped
2 red potatoes, boiled and shredded
1/2 lb. fresh crabmeat
1/2 c. dry bread crumbs
2 t. vegetable oil

In a medium bowl, combine mayonnaise, hot pepper sauce, egg whites, mustard, lemon zest, lemon juice and salt. Add celery, parsley, onions, potatoes and crabmeat; stir well. Make 6 cakes out of mixture and dredge through bread crumbs. In non-stick skillet, heat 1 teaspoon oil over medium heat. Cook 3 cakes at a time, adding remaining oil to skillet after first batch. Makes 6 crab cakes.

Quick, refreshing cooler...steep 8 mint teabags in 2 cups of boiling water. Add 2 cups of orange juice, 1 1/2 cups lemonade, 2 cups crushed ice and 2 cans of ginger ale. Garnish with orange slices.

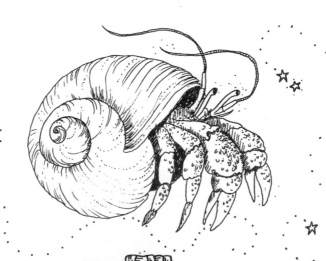

Cornmeal Biscuits

So tasty with any fish dish! Serve with butter and strawberry jam.

1/2 c. plus 2 T. skim milk	1 1/3 c. flour
2 T. vegetable oil	1 1/2 t. baking powder
1 egg, beaten	1 T. sugar
1/3 c. cornmeal	1/4 t. salt

Spray cookie sheet with vegetable cooking spray. Preheat oven to 400 degrees. In small bowl, whisk together milk, oil and egg. In large bowl combine cornmeal, flour, baking powder, sugar and salt. Add liquid ingredients, stirring until just moistened. Drop by teaspoonful onto cookie sheet, and bake 12 minutes until lightly browned. Makes 1 dozen biscuits.

For a nautical theme, use lengths of thick, white sailing rope to tie around napkins and silverware.

Blueberry-Lemon Mousse

Lemon and blueberries make a refreshing combination...include a lemon crunch cookie with each serving (recipe next page).

1 qt. freshly-picked blueberries, rinsed
1 c. sugar
1/2 t. cinnamon
5 large eggs, separated

juice of 2 lemons
1 c. heavy cream
2 t. lemon peel, grated

Combine berries with 1/4 cup of the sugar and refrigerate until ready to use. Beat egg yolks with remaining sugar and cinnamon until light yellow in color and add the lemon juice. Cook and whisk constantly in a double boiler over barely simmering water until mixture is thick enough to coat a spoon. Set aside. Beat egg whites until they form peaks. Fold egg whites into the egg yolk mixture. Whip the cream and fold into the egg mixture along with the lemon peel. Cover and chill at least one hour. Spoon mousse into serving bowls and top with the sugared berries.

Serve mousse, puddings and ice cream in individual shortcake cups you can buy at the grocery. Yum!

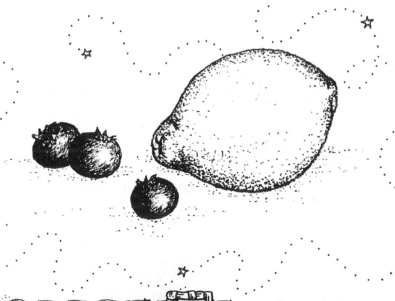

Lemon Crunch Cookies

Serve with blueberry-lemon mousse and minty iced tea.

1 c. flour	1 T. lemon zest
1/4 t. cream of tartar	1 egg
1/2 t. baking soda	1/4 t. allspice
1/4 c. margarine, softened	1/4 t. salt
3/4 c. sugar	1 c. quick oats
1 t. lemon juice	

Preheat oven to 350 degrees. In bowl, mix flour, cream of tartar and baking soda; set aside. Cream margarine and gradually add sugar. Beat at medium speed until well blended. Add lemon juice, lemon zest, egg, allspice and salt; beat well. Gradually add flour mixture and mix until combined. Stir in oatmeal. Drop dough by teaspoonfuls onto cookie sheets, and bake for 12 minutes. Makes 3 1/2 dozen.

Vary this recipe by using orange juice and orange zest and adding walnuts. Yum!

Seaside Clambake

Magical Ideas...

Summer Hanging Basket

A hanging basket will enhance your summer space, whether you're in a cottage on the seashore or the front porch in the Midwest. You'll need a 20-inch wire basket, moss, a plastic saucer, potting soil and your plants. Choose your plants early in the season to get the best selection and the healthiest plants. Be sure to buy enough to fill your basket, and select a variety of shapes and sizes to make your basket interesting. Before you begin, gently separate your moss so it will be easier to handle, and water all of your plants thoroughly. Line the basket about 3 inches deep with the moss, and place the saucer in the middle to help retain water. Place the trailing plants, such as ivy, vinca vine and lobelia, around the outer edge, pushing them through the openings in the basket. Their roots should rest in the saucer and be covered with potting soil. Add more soil to the center, and more moss around the edges as the remaining plants are tucked in. Add some bushy ones around the edge, and put the tall ones in the middle. Make sure all roots are covered with potting soil; then water thoroughly and hang.

Lavender Stars

Fragrant and pretty. Hang the stars in bedroom, bathroom or closet. They make a lovely hostess or shower gift.

6-inch length of 1/2 inch thick styrofoam
star-shaped metal cookie cutter
white craft glue
2 c. lavender blossoms, dried

variety of small, dried flowers such as rosebuds and baby's breath
2 florist's pins
1 yd. 1/4" satin ribbon

With the cookie cutter, cut two star shapes into the styrofoam; then coat both sides of each with glue. Roll gently in lavender blossoms and let dry. When completely dry, glue the small, dried flowers in a pleasing arrangement on one side of each star. With the florist's pins, fasten the ends of the ribbon to the back of each star. Add a drop of essential oil for extra fragrance, and they're ready to hang.

Seaside Garland

Beachcombers will love to make this unique strand of sea treasures. Collect seashells of all sizes and varieties, starfish, dried seaweed, small pieces of driftwood and worn bottle glass. Thread a strong, blunt needle with 36 inches of wire. Some shells will have holes already worn into them; other pieces may need to be drilled with a small electric drill. String your treasures along the garland and knot the end. Hang over your mantel for an instant memory.

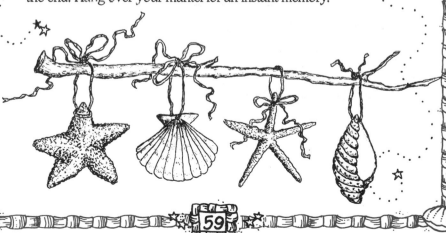

Birdbath End Table

Add some summer whimsy to your sunroom or screened-in porch.

plaster birdbath
1/4" glass to fit birdbath
dark green latex paint
white staining glaze

foam paintbrush
dried flowers, seashells or
colorful stones

Measure the width of the birdbath bowl just below the lip. Have glass cut to fit your measurement. Paint the birdbath with green paint and let dry. Use the roller to apply white glaze over the entire birdbath, highlighting the texture. When dry, fill the bowl with an arrangement of flowers, shells or stones and place glass on top.

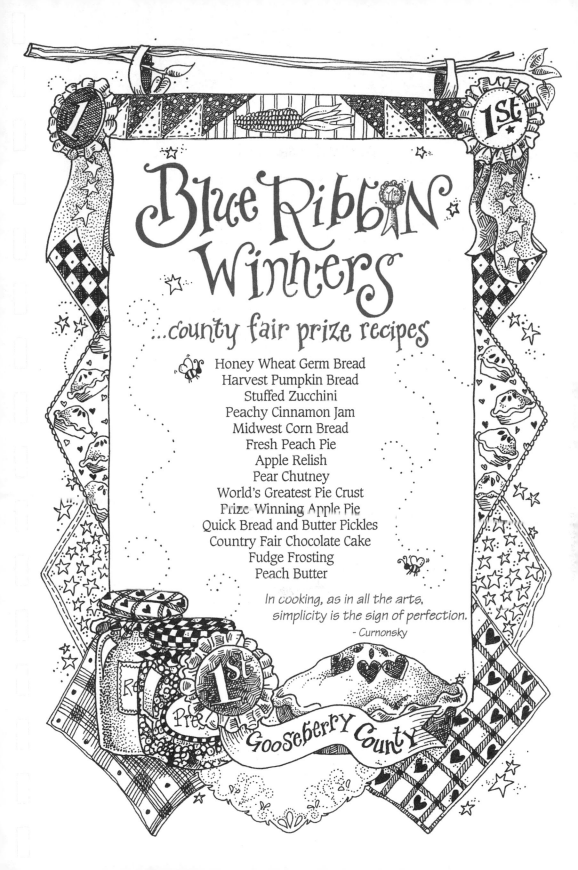

Blue Ribbon Winners

...county fair prize recipes

Honey Wheat Germ Bread
Harvest Pumpkin Bread
Stuffed Zucchini
Peachy Cinnamon Jam
Midwest Corn Bread
Fresh Peach Pie
Apple Relish
Pear Chutney
World's Greatest Pie Crust
Prize Winning Apple Pie
Quick Bread and Butter Pickles
Country Fair Chocolate Cake
Fudge Frosting
Peach Butter

In cooking, as in all the arts,
simplicity is the sign of perfection.
- Curnonsky

Gooseberry County

Honey Wheat Germ Bread

More than anything, it's the old-fashioned taste of home.

2 pkgs. dry yeast	1/4 c. honey
1 c. warm water	1 3/4 c. milk, scalded and
4 c. flour	cooled slightly
2 T. brown sugar	1 3/4 c. whole wheat flour
2 t. salt	1/4 c. wheat germ

Grease 2 standard loaf pans. Preheat oven to 375 degrees. In large mixing bowl combine yeast, water, 1/2 cup of flour, brown sugar, and salt; beat until smooth. Let stand covered in a warm place for 15 minutes. Add honey, milk, wheat flour and wheat germ. Beat 2 minutes with mixer and gradually add white flour. Fold out onto floured surface and shape into smooth ball. Cover with mixing bowl and let stand 10 minutes. Knead thoroughly and divide into 2 balls. Cover and let rest again. Shape each ball into a loaf and place in pans. In warm place, cover and let rise until doubled. Bake for 35 to 40 minutes.

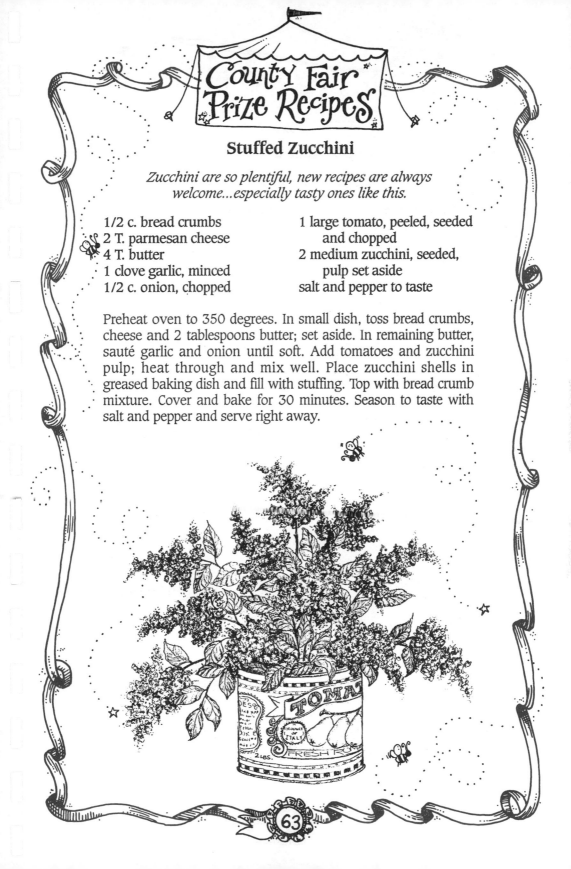

County Fair Prize Recipes

Stuffed Zucchini

Zucchini are so plentiful, new recipes are always welcome...especially tasty ones like this.

1/2 c. bread crumbs
2 T. parmesan cheese
4 T. butter
1 clove garlic, minced
1/2 c. onion, chopped
1 large tomato, peeled, seeded and chopped
2 medium zucchini, seeded, pulp set aside
salt and pepper to taste

Preheat oven to 350 degrees. In small dish, toss bread crumbs, cheese and 2 tablespoons butter; set aside. In remaining butter, sauté garlic and onion until soft. Add tomatoes and zucchini pulp; heat through and mix well. Place zucchini shells in greased baking dish and fill with stuffing. Top with bread crumb mixture. Cover and bake for 30 minutes. Season to taste with salt and pepper and serve right away.

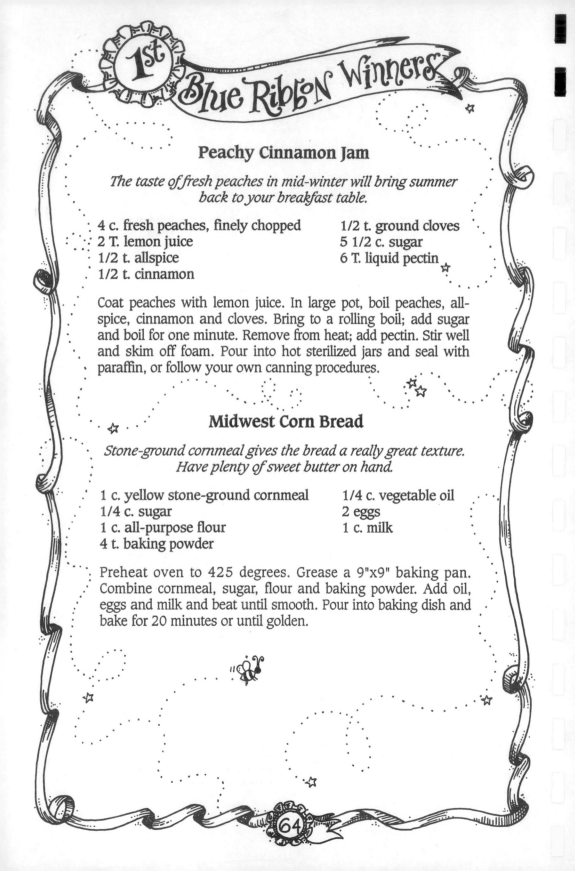

Peachy Cinnamon Jam

The taste of fresh peaches in mid-winter will bring summer back to your breakfast table.

4 c. fresh peaches, finely chopped
2 T. lemon juice
1/2 t. allspice
1/2 t. cinnamon

1/2 t. ground cloves
5 1/2 c. sugar
6 T. liquid pectin

Coat peaches with lemon juice. In large pot, boil peaches, all-spice, cinnamon and cloves. Bring to a rolling boil; add sugar and boil for one minute. Remove from heat; add pectin. Stir well and skim off foam. Pour into hot sterilized jars and seal with paraffin, or follow your own canning procedures.

Midwest Corn Bread

Stone-ground cornmeal gives the bread a really great texture. Have plenty of sweet butter on hand.

1 c. yellow stone-ground cornmeal
1/4 c. sugar
1 c. all-purpose flour
4 t. baking powder

1/4 c. vegetable oil
2 eggs
1 c. milk

Preheat oven to 425 degrees. Grease a 9"x9" baking pan. Combine cornmeal, sugar, flour and baking powder. Add oil, eggs and milk and beat until smooth. Pour into baking dish and bake for 20 minutes or until golden.

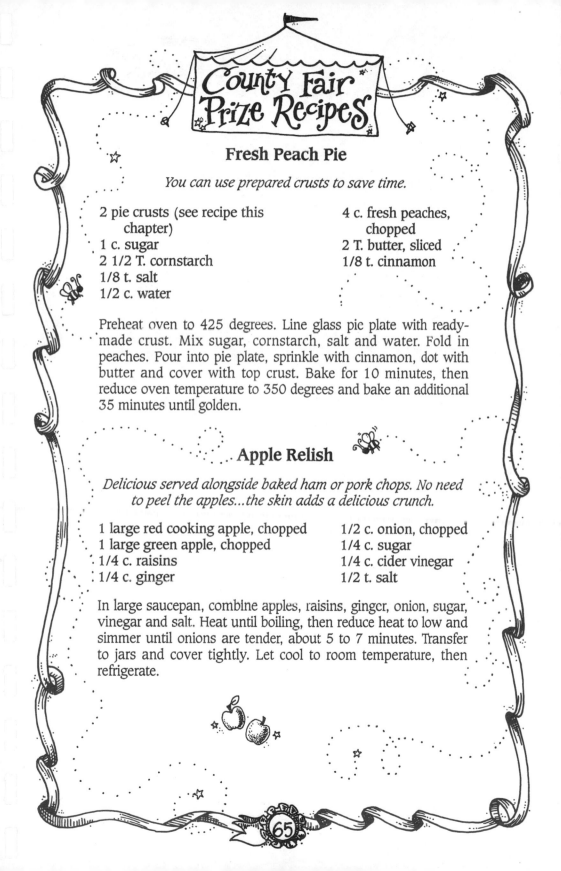

County Fair Prize Recipes

Fresh Peach Pie

You can use prepared crusts to save time.

2 pie crusts (see recipe this
    chapter)
1 c. sugar
2 1/2 T. cornstarch
1/8 t. salt
1/2 c. water

4 c. fresh peaches,
    chopped
2 T. butter, sliced
1/8 t. cinnamon

Preheat oven to 425 degrees. Line glass pic plate with ready-made crust. Mix sugar, cornstarch, salt and water. Fold in peaches. Pour into pie plate, sprinkle with cinnamon, dot with butter and cover with top crust. Bake for 10 minutes, then reduce oven temperature to 350 degrees and bake an additional 35 minutes until golden.

Apple Relish

Delicious served alongside baked ham or pork chops. No need to peel the apples...the skin adds a delicious crunch.

1 large red cooking apple, chopped
1 large green apple, chopped
1/4 c. raisins
1/4 c. ginger

1/2 c. onion, chopped
1/4 c. sugar
1/4 c. cider vinegar
1/2 t. salt

In large saucepan, combine apples, raisins, ginger, onion, sugar, vinegar and salt. Heat until boiling, then reduce heat to low and simmer until onions are tender, about 5 to 7 minutes. Transfer to jars and cover tightly. Let cool to room temperature, then refrigerate.

Pear Chutney

"Gourmet"-style preserves make beautiful holiday gifts.

5 c. pears, peeled, seeded and chopped

3 apples, peeled, seeded and chopped

2 lemons, seeded and chopped

2 tomatoes, peeled and chopped

1 lime, seeded and chopped

3 1/2 t. dried red pepper, crushed

3 c. brown sugar, packed

1 1/2 c. raisins

3 peaches, peeled, pitted and chopped

1 t. cinnamon

1 t. cloves

1/4 t. nutmeg

1/2 c. crystallized ginger

In large pot, combine all ingredients and simmer for 2 1/2 hours. Pack into sterilized jars according to the manufacturer's directions.

Neither a lofty degree of intelligence nor imagination nor both together go to the making of genius. Love, love, love, that is the soul of genius.
- Wolfgang Amadeus Mozart

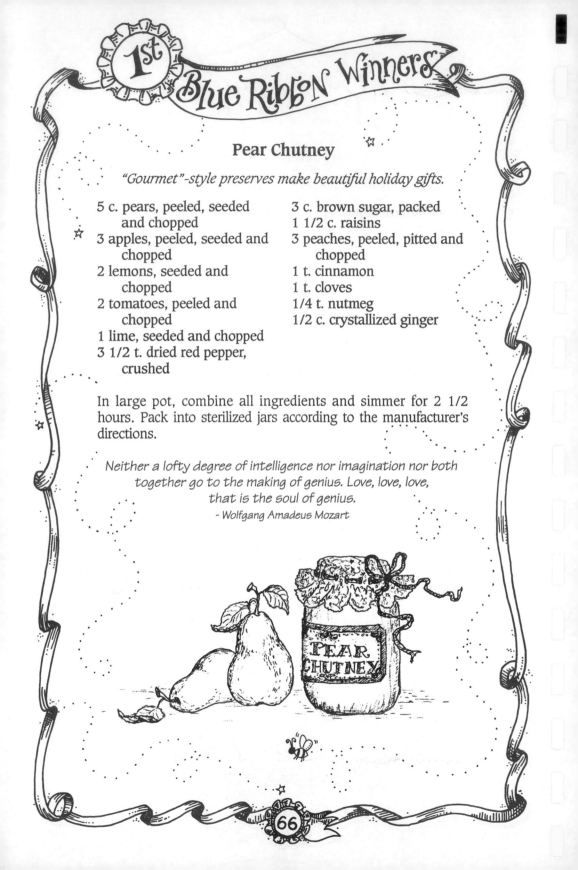

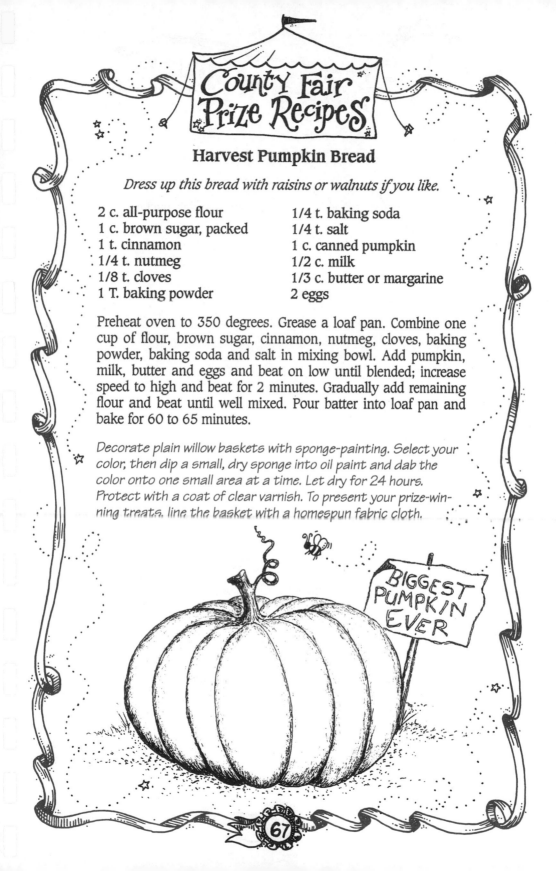

Harvest Pumpkin Bread

Dress up this bread with raisins or walnuts if you like.

2 c. all-purpose flour	1/4 t. baking soda
1 c. brown sugar, packed	1/4 t. salt
1 t. cinnamon	1 c. canned pumpkin
1/4 t. nutmeg	1/2 c. milk
1/8 t. cloves	1/3 c. butter or margarine
1 T. baking powder	2 eggs

Preheat oven to 350 degrees. Grease a loaf pan. Combine one cup of flour, brown sugar, cinnamon, nutmeg, cloves, baking powder, baking soda and salt in mixing bowl. Add pumpkin, milk, butter and eggs and beat on low until blended; increase speed to high and beat for 2 minutes. Gradually add remaining flour and beat until well mixed. Pour batter into loaf pan and bake for 60 to 65 minutes.

Decorate plain willow baskets with sponge-painting. Select your color, then dip a small, dry sponge into oil paint and dab the color onto one small area at a time. Let dry for 24 hours. Protect with a coat of clear varnish. To present your prize-winning treats, line the basket with a homespun fabric cloth.

BIGGEST PUMPKIN EVER

World's Greatest Pie Crust

Make crusts ahead of time and freeze (unbaked) in pans.
Great to pull out, fill and bake for fresh pie anytime!

1 3/4 c. shortening
5 c. flour
1 t. salt

1 egg, slightly beaten
1/4 c. ice water
1 T. vinegar

In mixing bowl, blend shortening, flour and salt with pastry blender until crumbly. Stir in egg, water and vinegar. Divide dough into 5 equal portions and roll out each onto floured surface. Makes 5 crusts.

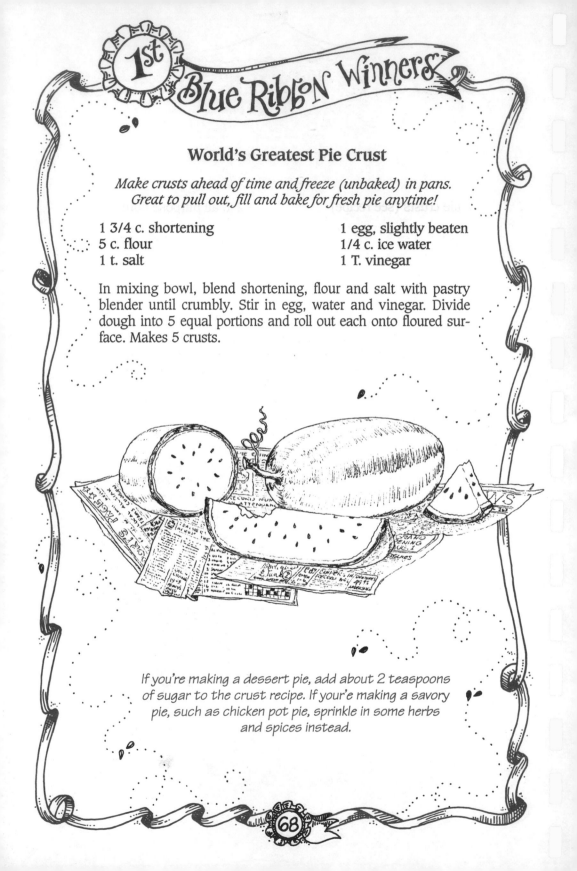

If you're making a dessert pie, add about 2 teaspoons of sugar to the crust recipe. If your'e making a savory pie, such as chicken pot pie, sprinkle in some herbs and spices instead.

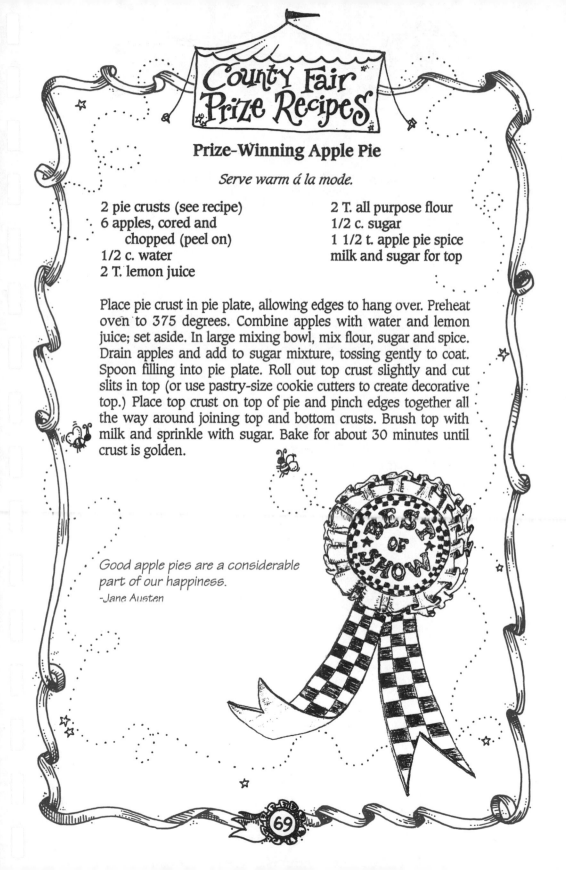

Prize-Winning Apple Pie

Serve warm á la mode.

2 pie crusts (see recipe)
6 apples, cored and
   chopped (peel on)
1/2 c. water
2 T. lemon juice

2 T. all purpose flour
1/2 c. sugar
1 1/2 t. apple pie spice
milk and sugar for top

Place pie crust in pie plate, allowing edges to hang over. Preheat oven to 375 degrees. Combine apples with water and lemon juice; set aside. In large mixing bowl, mix flour, sugar and spice. Drain apples and add to sugar mixture, tossing gently to coat. Spoon filling into pie plate. Roll out top crust slightly and cut slits in top (or use pastry-size cookie cutters to create decorative top.) Place top crust on top of pie and pinch edges together all the way around joining top and bottom crusts. Brush top with milk and sprinkle with sugar. Bake for about 30 minutes until crust is golden.

Good apple pies are a considerable part of our happiness.
-Jane Austen

Quick Bread and Butter Pickles

*This recipe gets a blue ribbon for homemade taste
without the fuss!*

1 qt. jar whole kosher dill
   pickles, store-bought
1 1/2 c. sugar
1 small onion, sliced

2 cinnamon sticks
2 T. vinegar

Drain pickles and cut into chunks 1/2 to 1 inch thick; place in
clean jar. Combine sugar, onion, cinnamon sticks and vinegar;
pour over pickles. Cover and refrigerate. Stir mixture once a day
for 2 to 3 days. Your "homemade" pickles are ready to serve
after 3 or 4 days.

*How to pick a prize watermelon? Of course, size is very impor-
tant! The best melons are firm, symmetrical and heavy for their
size and shape. The underside of a watermelon should be yellow.
If the melon responds with a hollow thump when you tap it, it's a
good sign that it's ripe. Whole watermelons should be stored in
the fridge. Cut pieces need to be tightly wrapped.*

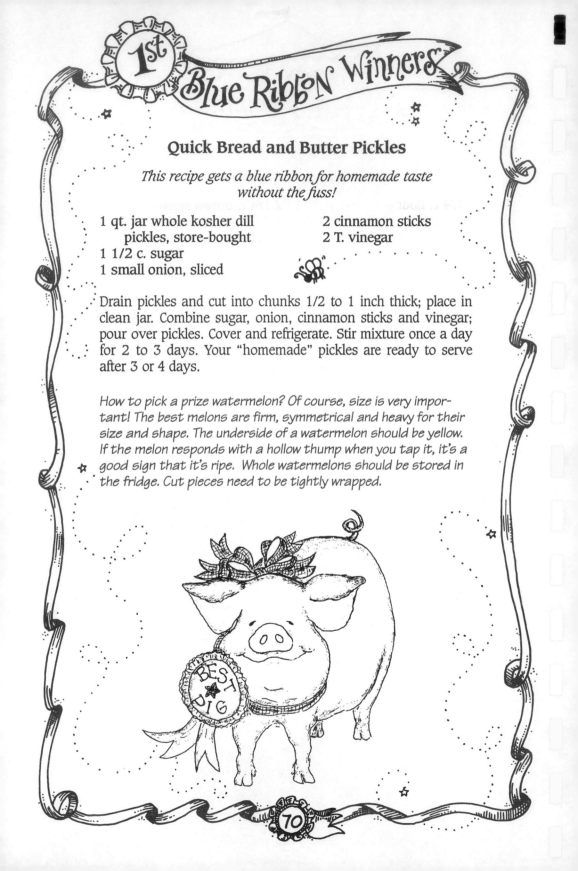

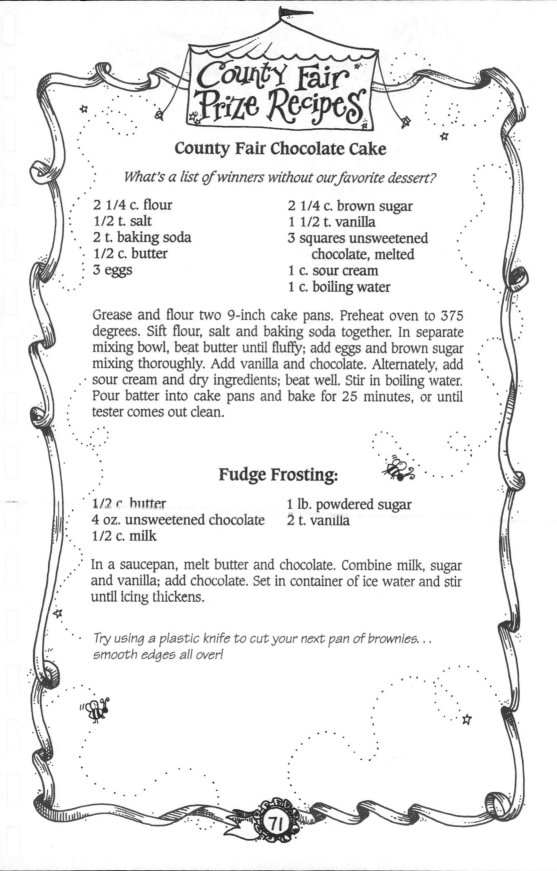

County Fair Prize Recipes

County Fair Chocolate Cake

What's a list of winners without our favorite dessert?

2 1/4 c. flour	2 1/4 c. brown sugar
1/2 t. salt	1 1/2 t. vanilla
2 t. baking soda	3 squares unsweetened
1/2 c. butter	chocolate, melted
3 eggs	1 c. sour cream
	1 c. boiling water

Grease and flour two 9-inch cake pans. Preheat oven to 375 degrees. Sift flour, salt and baking soda together. In separate mixing bowl, beat butter until fluffy; add eggs and brown sugar mixing thoroughly. Add vanilla and chocolate. Alternately, add sour cream and dry ingredients; beat well. Stir in boiling water. Pour batter into cake pans and bake for 25 minutes, or until tester comes out clean.

Fudge Frosting:

1/2 c. butter	1 lb. powdered sugar
4 oz. unsweetened chocolate	2 t. vanilla
1/2 c. milk	

In a saucepan, melt butter and chocolate. Combine milk, sugar and vanilla; add chocolate. Set in container of ice water and stir until icing thickens.

Try using a plastic knife to cut your next pan of brownies. . . smooth edges all over!

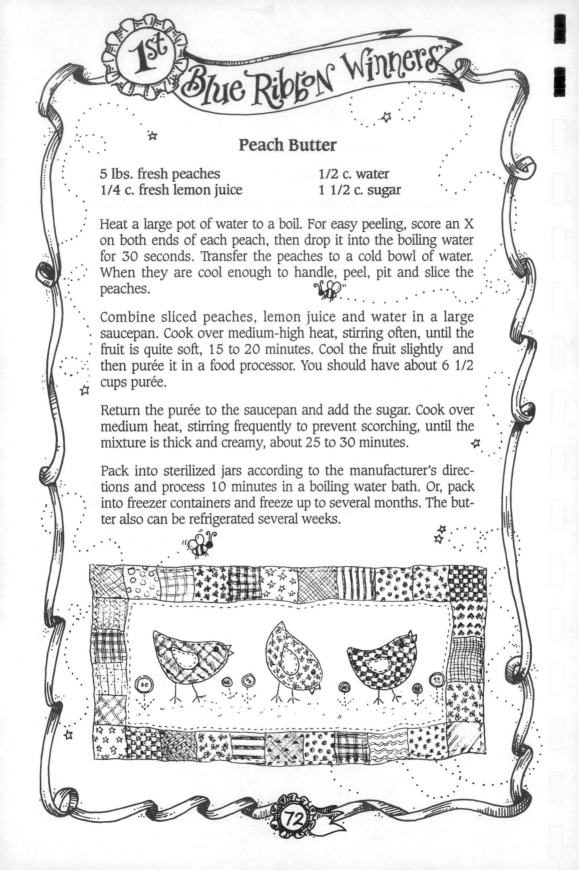

Peach Butter

5 lbs. fresh peaches   1/2 c. water
1/4 c. fresh lemon juice   1 1/2 c. sugar

Heat a large pot of water to a boil. For easy peeling, score an X on both ends of each peach, then drop it into the boiling water for 30 seconds. Transfer the peaches to a cold bowl of water. When they are cool enough to handle, peel, pit and slice the peaches.

Combine sliced peaches, lemon juice and water in a large saucepan. Cook over medium-high heat, stirring often, until the fruit is quite soft, 15 to 20 minutes. Cool the fruit slightly and then purée it in a food processor. You should have about 6 1/2 cups purée.

Return the purée to the saucepan and add the sugar. Cook over medium heat, stirring frequently to prevent scorching, until the mixture is thick and creamy, about 25 to 30 minutes.

Pack into sterilized jars according to the manufacturer's directions and process 10 minutes in a boiling water bath. Or, pack into freezer containers and freeze up to several months. The butter also can be refrigerated several weeks.

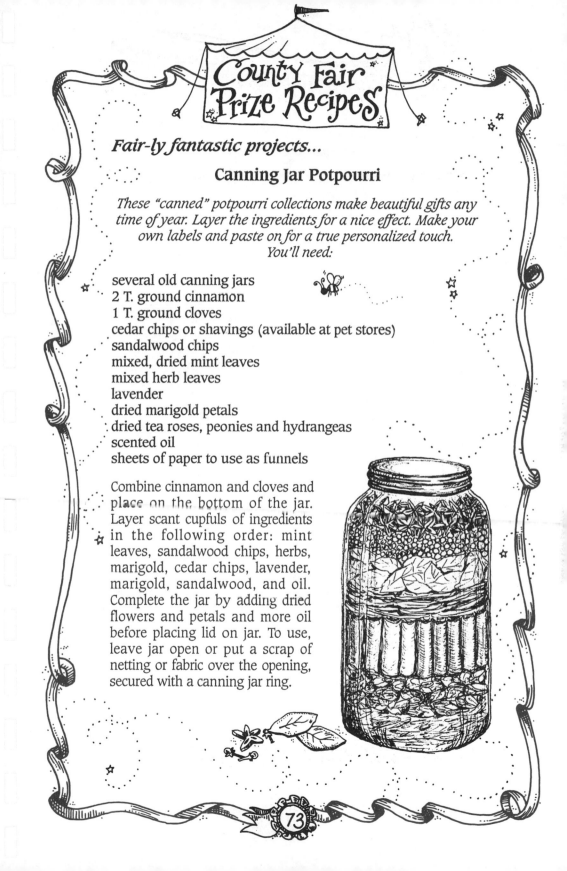

County Fair Prize Recipes

Fair-ly fantastic projects...

Canning Jar Potpourri

These "canned" potpourri collections make beautiful gifts any time of year. Layer the ingredients for a nice effect. Make your own labels and paste on for a true personalized touch.
You'll need:

several old canning jars
2 T. ground cinnamon
1 T. ground cloves
cedar chips or shavings (available at pet stores)
sandalwood chips
mixed, dried mint leaves
mixed herb leaves
lavender
dried marigold petals
dried tea roses, peonies and hydrangeas
scented oil
sheets of paper to use as funnels

Combine cinnamon and cloves and place on the bottom of the jar. Layer scant cupfuls of ingredients in the following order: mint leaves, sandalwood chips, herbs, marigold, cedar chips, lavender, marigold, sandalwood, and oil. Complete the jar by adding dried flowers and petals and more oil before placing lid on jar. To use, leave jar open or put a scrap of netting or fabric over the opening, secured with a canning jar ring.

Prize Keepsake Box

Perfect for any gift occasion...fill with treats or use for post cards, letters, photos, even the blue ribbon for your first prize bread and butter pickles! You can use any stencil design... we used a heart design for ours.

wooden Shaker box
heart stencil
stencil brush
red acrylic paint
fine sandpaper

masking tape
varnish
permanent felt-tip
   fine-point marker
paper towels

Place heart stencil in center of box and keep in place with tape. Dip clean, dry stencil brush into red paint, tap on paper towel until almost dry, then stencil heart on the box. Allow paint to dry slightly before removing stencil. When paint is dry, write a sentiment along the inside or outside edge of the heart. Ideas might include: "Heart of the home," "Close to my heart," or "Heart-felt thanks." You'll want to vary your sentiment depending on the stencil you use. When dry, add two coats of varnish and allow to cure for 24 hours.

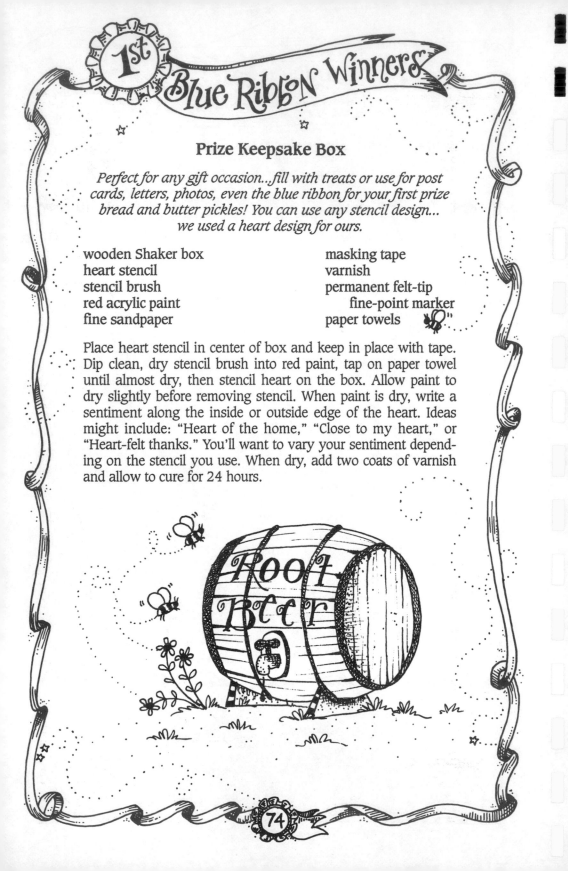

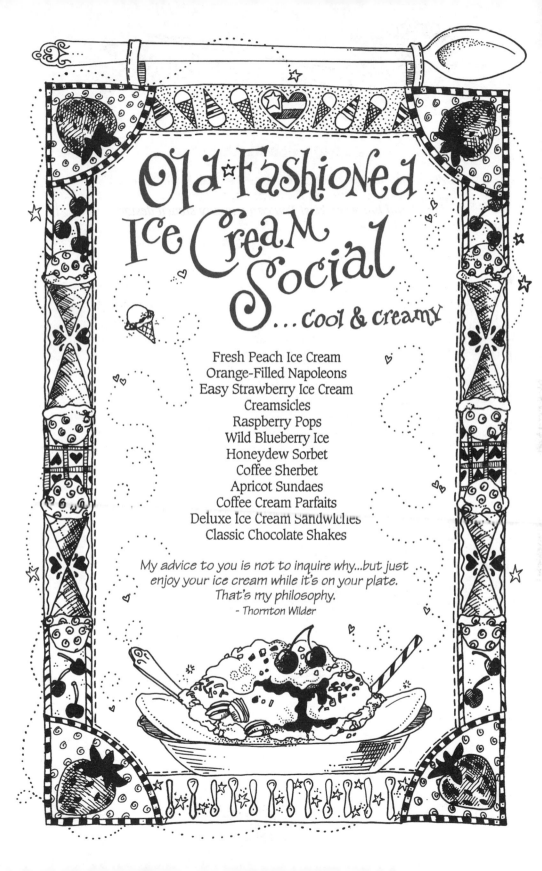

Old-Fashioned Ice Cream Social

...cool & creamy

Fresh Peach Ice Cream
Orange-Filled Napoleons
Easy Strawberry Ice Cream
Creamsicles
Raspberry Pops
Wild Blueberry Ice
Honeydew Sorbet
Coffee Sherbet
Apricot Sundaes
Coffee Cream Parfaits
Deluxe Ice Cream Sandwiches
Classic Chocolate Shakes

*My advice to you is not to inquire why...but just
enjoy your ice cream while it's on your plate.
That's my philosophy.*
- Thornton Wilder

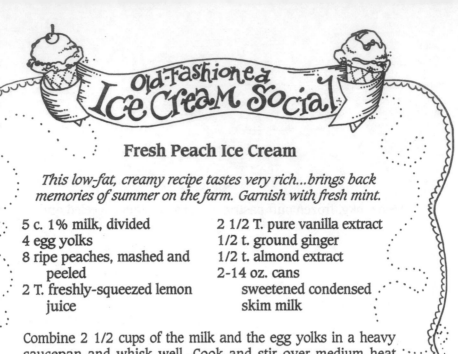

Fresh Peach Ice Cream

This low-fat, creamy recipe tastes very rich...brings back memories of summer on the farm. Garnish with fresh mint.

5 c. 1% milk, divided
4 egg yolks
8 ripe peaches, mashed and peeled
2 T. freshly-squeezed lemon juice

2 1/2 T. pure vanilla extract
1/2 t. ground ginger
1/2 t. almond extract
2-14 oz. cans sweetened condensed skim milk

Combine 2 1/2 cups of the milk and the egg yolks in a heavy saucepan and whisk well. Cook and stir over medium heat about 10 minutes, or until mixture will coat a spoon. (Do not overcook, or it will turn into scrambled eggs!) Combine egg mixture with remaining milk, peaches and all remaining ingredients in a large bowl and stir well. Cover and chill. Pour mixture into the freezer section of an ice cream freezer. Freeze according to manufacturer's directions. Spoon into a container with a tight-fitting lid and freeze for an hour, or until completely firm. Serves 12 - 24, depending on size of serving!

I scream, you scream, we all scream for ice cream!
- Children's rhyme

cool & creamy

Orange-filled Napoleons

Easy to make and elegant to serve!

8 oz. pkg. frozen puff pastry
    sheets, thawed
2 c. softened vanilla ice
    cream

1 naval orange, peeled and
    thinly sliced
powdered sugar

Preheat oven to 375 degrees. Unfold pastry and cut into 8 rectangles. Place on ungreased cookie sheet and bake for 20 minutes or until pastries are puffed and golden. Cool on wire rack. To serve, split pastries lengthwise. Spoon ice cream on one half; top with orange slices and replace pastry top. Dust with powdered sugar and serve immediately.

*A swarm of bees in May
Is worth a load of hay;
A swarm of bees in June
Is worth a silver spoon;
A swarm of bees in July
Is not worth a fly.*
- Old English proverb

Easy Strawberry Ice Cream

Garnish with a ripe red strawberry and a wafer cookie. Vary the recipe with different fruits throughout the summer.

2/3 c. very cold buttermilk
1 t. orange extract

2-10 oz. pkgs. frozen strawberries, slightly thawed

Place buttermilk and orange extract into blender or food processor. Cut slightly thawed fruit into chunks and add to blender. Whirl until mixture is smooth and ice cream consistency. Serve immediately.

Bake a batch of your favorite cookies...chocolate chip, peanut butter, oatmeal, sugar...and sandwich different flavors of ice cream inside. Yum!

YUMMY CO

cool & creamy

Creamsicles

*Pure orange juice makes these taste so much
better than store-bought.*

1 pt. vanilla ice cream or ice
  milk, softened
6 oz. can frozen orange juice
  concentrate, thawed

1/4 c. honey
1 1/2 c. skim milk

In large bowl, mix together ice cream, orange juice concentrate
and honey. Gradually beat in milk. Freeze in small waxed paper
cups or ice cube tray. Insert sticks into paper cup molds when
partially frozen. Makes 12 creamsicles.

Raspberry Pops

*Try making these pops with blackberries or strawberries
for a nice variety!*

1/4 c. honey
8 oz. pkg. cream cheese,
  softened
1 c. bananas, sliced
10 oz. pkg. frozen raspberries,
  slightly thawed

1 c. heavy cream, whipped
2 c. miniature marshmallows
10-5 oz. paper drinking cups
10 wooden treat sticks

Gradually add honey to cream cheese, mixing until well blended. Stir in fruit; fold in whipped cream and marshmallows. Pour
into paper cups; insert wooden sticks in center and freeze until
firm. Peel away cups and enjoy! Makes 10 pops.

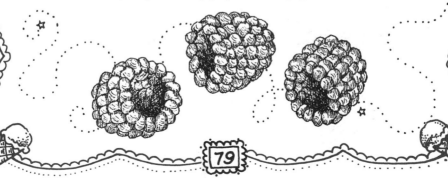

Wild Blueberry Ice

We're using frozen blueberries for ease of preparation...you can use fresh blueberries that you've simmered and stirred in a small amount of water and allowed to cool.

1/4 c. sugar
1/2 c. water
15 oz. pkg. frozen blueberries in heavy syrup, thawed and syrup drained (reserve syrup)

In small saucepan, cook sugar and water over low heat until sugar dissolves. Remove from heat; add syrup from blueberries and half of the berries. Chill thoroughly. Freeze mixture in an ice cream maker according to manufacturer's instructions. Serve right away topped with remaining blueberries.

Make an ice cream "watermelon"...line a big bowl with softened pistachio ice cream (this will be the rind), and set aside in freezer. Fold chocolate chips (for the seeds) into softened strawberry ice cream. Pour the strawberry ice cream into the bowl over the pistachio layer. Place bowl in the freezer. To serve, just remove ice cream from bowl and slice into watermelon-shaped wedges.

cool & creamy

Honeydew Sorbet

You can also make this recipe with cantaloupe. Delicious!

2 lbs. honeydew melon,
    peeled and seeded
1/2 c. sweet dessert wine

1/2 c. sugar
1/4 t. ground cinnamon

Cut melon into large pieces and purée in
blender. Add wine, sugar and cinnamon
and blend until sugar dissolves.
Pour mixture into an ice cream
maker and process according
to directions. Freeze in a
tightly-covered container.

Coffee Sherbet

*Try this recipe with a
variety of flavored
coffees...vanilla, almond,
hazelnut...mmm!*

2/3 c. sugar
4 c. strong coffee,
    hot and freshly brewed
1/2 c. milk

Combine sugar and hot coffee until sugar dissolves. Add milk
and chill thoroughly. Freeze in an ice cream maker according to
manufacturer's instructions, and serve immediately.

The only emperor is the emperor of ice cream.
- Wallace Stevens

Apricot Sundaes

Your favorite vanilla ice cream serves as a base for this delicious fruity sundae.

12 oz. jar apricot preserves
1 1/2 t. lemon zest, grated
1/3 c. unsweetened pineapple juice

1/3 c. brown sugar,
firmly packed

Combine all ingredients in bowl and microwave on high for 2 minutes. Stir until sugar is dissolved and serve warm over vanilla ice cream.

In the morning, very early,
That's the time I love to go
Barefoot where the fern grows curly
And grass is cool between each toe,
On a summer morning-O!
On a summer morning.
- Rachel Field

cool & creamy

Coffee Cream Parfaits

Sprinkle chocolate curls on top for an extra treat!

1 qt. vanilla ice cream, slightly thawed	1 1/2 t. sugar
1 c. coffee liqueur	1 1/2 t. instant
1/2 c. cream	espresso

In tall ice cream or parfait glasses, layer the ice cream and liqueur. Chill in freezer for a half an hour or more. When ready to serve, whip together cream, sugar and espresso until soft peaks form; top parfaits. Serves 4.

Deluxe Ice Cream Sandwiches

We like these chewy, thin oatmeal cookies.

Cookies:

1 1/2 c. sweet butter	1 3/4 c. sugar
3 c. uncooked rolled oats (not instant)	2 t. vanilla extract
1 1/2 T. flour	2 eggs, lightly beaten
1 t. salt	

Sandwiches:

1/2 gallon natural vanilla ice cream
sprinkles

Melt the butter in a large saucepan over low heat. Let cool and add oats, flour, salt, sugar and vanilla. Stir well to combine, then add eggs and mix thoroughly. On a baking sheet that has been covered with parchment and buttered, spoon 1 1/2 tablespoons of batter for each cook, leaving about 3 inches between cookies. Flatten cookies into circles. Bake until golden brown, about 15 minutes. Let cool. Makes 2 dozen. Unwrap a square block of vanilla ice cream and slice into 1-inch thick slices, cutting into squares big enough to slightly overlap edges of cookies. Sandwich ice cream between cookies. Dip edges of sandwiches into sprinkles. Wrap individually and freeze until ready to serve.

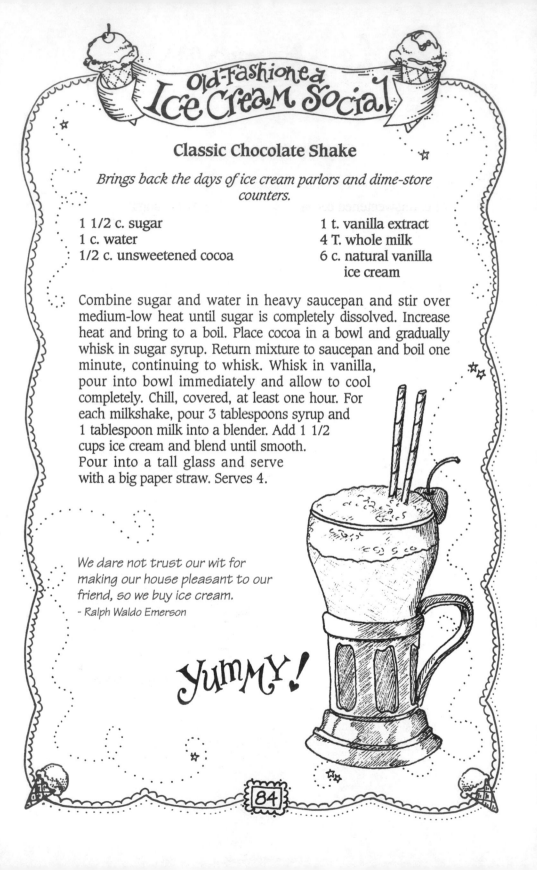

Classic Chocolate Shake

Brings back the days of ice cream parlors and dime-store counters.

1 1/2 c. sugar
1 c. water
1/2 c. unsweetened cocoa

1 t. vanilla extract
4 T. whole milk
6 c. natural vanilla
ice cream

Combine sugar and water in heavy saucepan and stir over medium-low heat until sugar is completely dissolved. Increase heat and bring to a boil. Place cocoa in a bowl and gradually whisk in sugar syrup. Return mixture to saucepan and boil one minute, continuing to whisk. Whisk in vanilla, pour into bowl immediately and allow to cool completely. Chill, covered, at least one hour. For each milkshake, pour 3 tablespoons syrup and 1 tablespoon milk into a blender. Add 1 1/2 cups ice cream and blend until smooth. Pour into a tall glass and serve with a big paper straw. Serves 4.

We dare not trust our wit for making our house pleasant to our friend, so we buy ice cream.
- Ralph Waldo Emerson

Yummy!

Tantalizing Toppings...

Hot Fudge

1/2 c. unsweetened cocoa
   powder
1 c. sour cream

1 1/2 c. sugar
1/2 t. vanilla extract

In a double boiler, combine all ingredients, stirring cocoa powder until well-mixed throughout. Cook over boiling water for about an hour, stirring until thick and creamy. Keep warm in a crock-pot set to low heat.

Blueberry Syrup

1 c. blueberries
1/2 c. sugar
1/4 vanilla bean, split
   lengthwise

3/4 c. water
2 1/2 T. freshly-squeezed
   lemon juice

Combine blueberries, sugar and vanilla bean in a medium saucepan. Add water and bring to a boil over medium-high heat. Reduce heat to low and simmer about 5 minutes. Remove vanilla bean and pour mixture into a blender. Add lemon juice and blend until smooth.

Strawberry Preserves

Serve over vanilla ice cream, or swirl into whipped cream for a strawberry "fool."

4 qts. small, ripe strawberries
9 c. sugar
juice of 1 lemon

Hull strawberries and layer them with sugar in a glass bowl. Cover and let stand overnight. Pour strawberry-sugar mixture into a deep, non-aluminum saucepan. Add lemon juice and heat to a boil. Let simmer 5 minutes. Return strawberry mixture to bowl, cover, and let stand 24 hours. Return strawberry mixture to pan and bring to a rapid boil until the syrup has thickened, about 30 minutes. Cool slightly. If not using right away, pack into sterilized jars according to the manufacturer's directions and process 10 minutes in a boiling water bath. Or, pack into freezer containers and freeze up to several months. The preserves can be refrigerated several weeks, if you don't intend to freeze them.

More Quick Topping Ideas

Crushed chocolate sandwich cookies
Peanuts, cashews or macadamia nuts
Colored sugar sprinkles
Chocolate jimmies
Crushed hard candies
Sweetened cocoa powder (fill a big shaker full)
Chocolate chips and chunks
Butterscotch chips
Whipped topping, colored with a few drops of food coloring
    just for fun
Fresh blueberries, strawberries, raspberries or blackberries
Honey
Crushed pineapple
...and don't forget the maraschino cherries!

Tex-Mex Feast

...spicy HOT stuff

Tortilla Roll-Ups
Pita Crisps
Nachos Magnifico
Chili Con Queso Dip
Tortilla Soup
Texas Border Barbecued Beef Ribs
Broiled Chicken Breasts with Lime
Spicy Grilled Vegetables
Fresh Corn-Tomato Salsa
Papaya Salsa
Peanut Butter Round-up Cookies
Iced Cowboy Coffee
Lone Star Pecan Cake

*Wish I had time
for just one more
bowl of chili.*
—Kit Carson

Tex-Mex Feast

Tortilla Roll-Ups

Have an extra stack of tortillas ready for make-your-own roll-ups.

8 oz. pkg. cream cheese,
   softened
4 oz. can green chilies,
   chopped
1 tomato, finely chopped

5 green onions, thinly sliced
2 oz. can black olives, sliced
5 soft flour tortillas

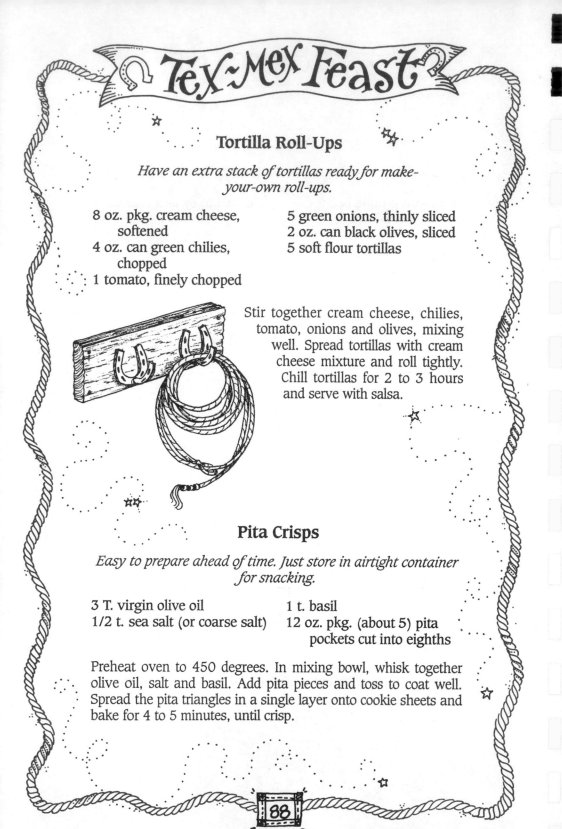

Stir together cream cheese, chilies, tomato, onions and olives, mixing well. Spread tortillas with cream cheese mixture and roll tightly. Chill tortillas for 2 to 3 hours and serve with salsa.

Pita Crisps

Easy to prepare ahead of time. Just store in airtight container for snacking.

3 T. virgin olive oil
1/2 t. sea salt (or coarse salt)

1 t. basil
12 oz. pkg. (about 5) pita
   pockets cut into eighths

Preheat oven to 450 degrees. In mixing bowl, whisk together olive oil, salt and basil. Add pita pieces and toss to coat well. Spread the pita triangles in a single layer onto cookie sheets and bake for 4 to 5 minutes, until crisp.

Spicy HOT stuff

Nachos Magnifico

Vary the ingredients according to your creativity and taste.

1 lb. lean ground beef
1 c. onions, chopped
salt and pepper, to taste
2-15 oz. cans refried beans
4 oz. can green chilies,
    chopped
1 c. cheddar cheese,
    shredded
1 c. mozzarella cheese,
    shredded

1 c. Monterey Jack cheese,
    shredded
6 oz. container guacamole
2 1/4 oz. can black olives,
    drained and sliced
1 c. green onion, chopped
1 1/2 c. sour cream
tortilla chips

Heat oven to 400 degrees. Lightly grease 13"x9" baking dish with cooking spray. In skillet, brown ground beef and onions; drain. Season with salt and pepper. Spread refried beans into bottom of baking dish and cover with beef. Layer on chilies and salsa. Sprinkle top with cheeses; cover and bake for 35 to 40 minutes. Top with guacamole, olives, onions, and sour cream. Serve right away with warm, crisp tortilla chips.

*...to get the full value
of a joy, you must
have somebody
to divide it with.*
- Mark Twain

☆ Tex-Mex Feast ☆

Chili Con Queso Dip

Serve with tortilla chips, crisp cold veggies and baked pita slices.

28 oz. can plum tomatoes, drained and chopped
2-4 oz. cans green chilies, drained and seeded
1 c. heavy cream

1 lb. cheddar cheese, shredded
salt and pepper, to taste

Over low heat, cook the tomatoes and chilies for about 15 minutes. Stirring constantly, add cream and cheese and continue cooking until mixture thickens. Season with salt and pepper and serve warm.

Wealth I ask not, hope nor love,
Nor a friend to know me;
All I ask, the heaven above
And the road below me.
- Robert Louis Stevenson

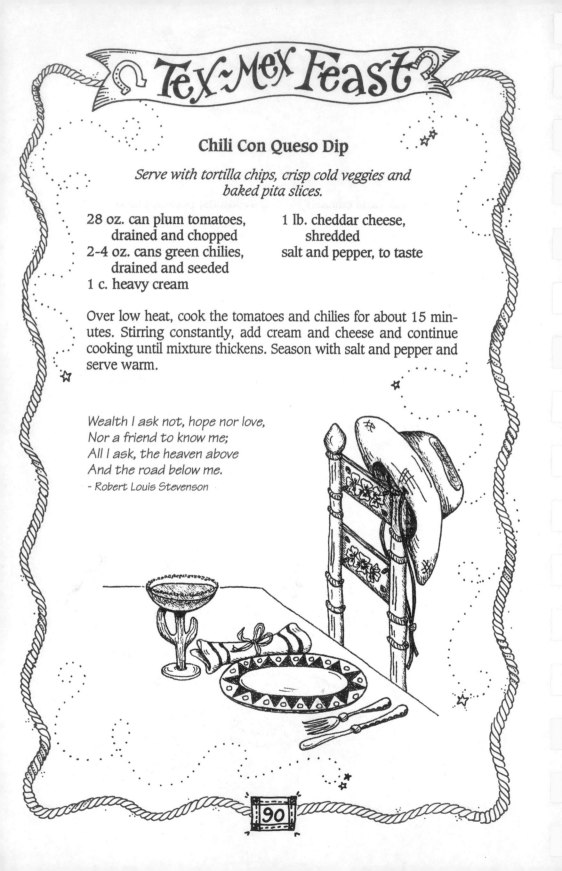

Tortilla Soup

For a heartier soup, add cubed chicken breasts.

6-14 1/2 oz. cans chicken broth
2-4 oz. cans mild green chilies
1/3 c. fresh mint leaves
1 t. chili powder
1 t. cumin
red pepper flakes to taste
2 cloves garlic, minced
1 c. fresh tomatoes, chopped

2 avocados, peeled, pitted and chopped
4 slices bacon, cooked, drained and crumbled
1/2 c. plus 2 T. fresh cilantro, chopped (reserve 2 T. for garnish)
sour cream (for garnish)
tortilla chips, slightly crushed

In large stockpot, combine chicken broth, chilies, mint leaves, chili powder, cumin, pepper and garlic; bring to a boil. Reduce heat to low and simmer for about 1 hour. In another bowl, while soup is simmering, combine tomatoes, avocados, bacon and cilantro. Strain broth, return to stockpot and boil again. To serve, add broth to individual soup bowls, place a scoopful of tomato mixture and top with tortilla chips. Garnish with sour cream and cilantro and serve right away. Serves 12.

Different-colored bandanas make colorful napkins for any barbecue. Tie one around each person's set of utensils. After the party, just toss them in the wash.

Texas Border Barbecued Beef Ribs

Make the chili sauce the night before to allow the flavors to ripen. Serve extra sauce at the table.

Red Chili Sauce:

2 T. shortening
2 T. flour
1/4 c. mild red chili pepper, ground
2 c. beef bouillon

1 clove garlic, minced
3/4 t. salt
1/4 t. cilantro,
    crushed
1/4 t. ground cumin

Melt shortening in a large saucepan over medium heat. Gradually add flour, stirring with a fork to mix thoroughly until flour turns golden brown. Remove pan from heat and stir in chili pepper, then bouillon. Return pan to heat and add remaining ingredients. Simmer, uncovered, 30 to 45 minutes. Adjust seasonings if necessary. Allow to cool, then refrigerate overnight. Makes 2 cups.

Marinade:

1/3 c. red chili sauce (above
    recipe)
1 c. dry red wine
2 T. olive oil
1 large clove garlic, minced

1 small yellow onion, diced
1/2 t. salt
freshly-ground black pepper
    to taste
4 lbs. beef short ribs

Combine all ingredients except ribs in a large mixing bowl and allow marinade to sit for 15 minutes to a half hour, letting flavors blend. Arrange ribs on a large roasting pan in a single layer. Pour marinade over the ribs, covering completely. Rub the marinade into the ribs. Position roasting rack about 3 inches above the coals. Remove ribs from the marinade and save marinade in a separate bowl. Place ribs directly on the grill and sear 10 minutes on a side. Remove ribs, raise rack another 2 inches, and cover with foil. With a fork, poke several holes in the foil for ventilation. Place ribs on the foil and cover with remaining marinade. Cook and turn the ribs every five minutes, basting often for about 40 minutes, until crusty and brown on the outside. Serves 4.

Broiled Chicken Breasts with Lime

Serve with a garnish of avocado and lime slices.

2 T. honey
3 T. lime juice
2 T. lime zest, grated
1/2 t. cumin

1/3 c. tequila
4 skinless, boneless
    chicken breasts

Preheat broiler and position rack about 4 inches below broiler. In medium bowl, whisk together honey, lime juice, lime zest, cumin and tequila. Dredge chicken breast through marinade to coat thoroughly. Broil for 6 to 8 minutes, turning once and basting several times.

Can't grill outside due to weather? Use your oven broiler, waiting until the last few minutes of cooking to baste meat and veggies.

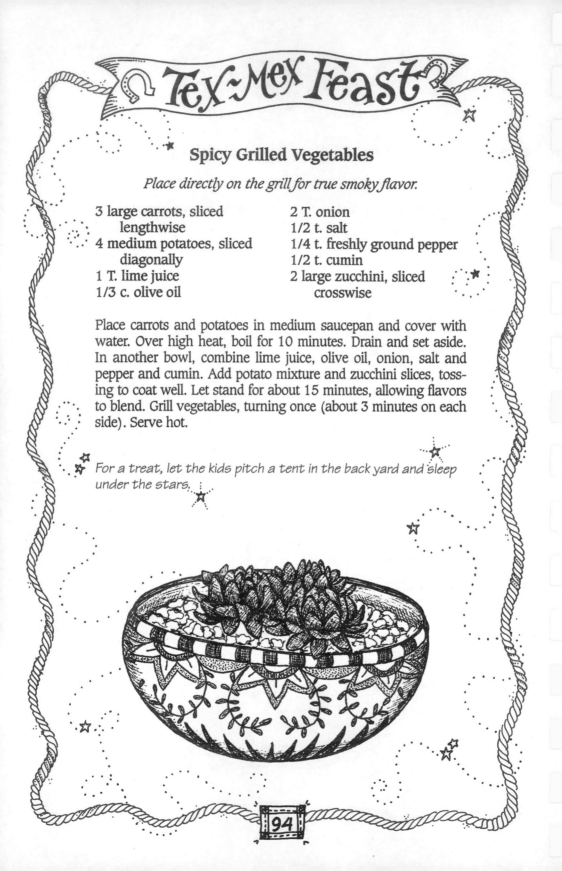

Tex~Mex Feast

Spicy Grilled Vegetables

Place directly on the grill for true smoky flavor.

3 large carrots, sliced
    lengthwise
4 medium potatoes, sliced
    diagonally
1 T. lime juice
1/3 c. olive oil

2 T. onion
1/2 t. salt
1/4 t. freshly ground pepper
1/2 t. cumin
2 large zucchini, sliced
    crosswise

Place carrots and potatoes in medium saucepan and cover with water. Over high heat, boil for 10 minutes. Drain and set aside. In another bowl, combine lime juice, olive oil, onion, salt and pepper and cumin. Add potato mixture and zucchini slices, tossing to coat well. Let stand for about 15 minutes, allowing flavors to blend. Grill vegetables, turning once (about 3 minutes on each side). Serve hot.

For a treat, let the kids pitch a tent in the back yard and sleep under the stars.

Fresh Corn-Tomato Salsa

A delicious, spicy chip dip...or spoon on top of Spanish rice.

1 c. fresh corn, cooked
1 large ripe tomato, peeled, seeded and chopped
1 small cucumber, peeled, seeded and chopped
1 small onion, finely chopped
1 small celery stalk, chopped

1 jalepeño pepper, chopped
3 T. lime juice, freshly-squeezed
1/2 t. cumin
1 large garlic clove, minced
1/2 t. salt

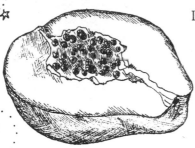

In medium bowl, stir together all ingredients until mixed well. Cover and refrigerate, allowing flavors to blend for at least an hour.

Papaya Salsa

Tasty salsa that can be prepared up to 3 days ahead of your party. Serve with chicken fajitas or blue corn chips.

1 medium ripe papaya
1/4 c. pineapple juice
6 T. lime juice
1 clove garlic, minced
1 small red bell pepper, chopped

1/4 c. fresh cilantro
1 small red onion, thinly sliced
1 small red pepper, diced
1 jalepeño pepper
salt and pepper to taste

Combine all ingredients well and chill, allowing flavors to blend.

"Salsa" is simply sauce! You can make a variety of salsas with a combination of sweet fruit and hot peppers. Experiment with watermelon, peaches or nectarines.

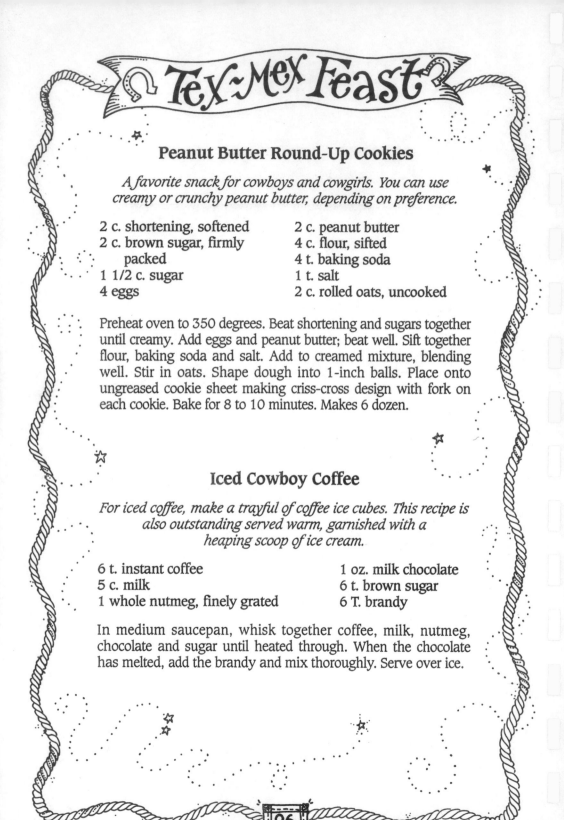

Tex-Mex Feast

Peanut Butter Round-Up Cookies

A favorite snack for cowboys and cowgirls. You can use creamy or crunchy peanut butter, depending on preference.

2 c. shortening, softened
2 c. brown sugar, firmly
   packed
1 1/2 c. sugar
4 eggs

2 c. peanut butter
4 c. flour, sifted
4 t. baking soda
1 t. salt
2 c. rolled oats, uncooked

Preheat oven to 350 degrees. Beat shortening and sugars together until creamy. Add eggs and peanut butter; beat well. Sift together flour, baking soda and salt. Add to creamed mixture, blending well. Stir in oats. Shape dough into 1-inch balls. Place onto ungreased cookie sheet making criss-cross design with fork on each cookie. Bake for 8 to 10 minutes. Makes 6 dozen.

Iced Cowboy Coffee

For iced coffee, make a trayful of coffee ice cubes. This recipe is also outstanding served warm, garnished with a heaping scoop of ice cream.

6 t. instant coffee
5 c. milk
1 whole nutmeg, finely grated

1 oz. milk chocolate
6 t. brown sugar
6 T. brandy

In medium saucepan, whisk together coffee, milk, nutmeg, chocolate and sugar until heated through. When the chocolate has melted, add the brandy and mix thoroughly. Serve over ice.

Spicy HOT stuff

Lone Star Pecan Cake

So rich, it needs no frosting. Dust with powdered sugar over a star stencil, just for fun.

1 lb. sweet butter	4 c. unbleached flour
2 c. sugar	1 1/2 t. baking powder
6 eggs, well beaten	4 c. pecan halves
1 t. lemon extract	2 c. golden raisins

Grease and flour a 9-inch tube pan and preheat oven to 300 degrees. Blend butter and sugar in a large mixing bowl and beat until light and fluffy. Gradually add eggs and lemon, continuing to beat. Sift flour and baking powder together three times to mix thoroughly. Add nuts and raisins to the dry mixture. Gradually blend dry ingredients to creamed mixture and blend well. Pour into the prepared pan and bake for 1 1/2 to 2 hours, or until a toothpick comes out clean. Cool for 15 minutes, then remove from pan. Dust with powdered sugar.

Best of the West...

Southwest Chili Garland

A fun decoration with true southwestern flair. You'll need a large-eyed needle, such as a tapestry needle, 36 inches of strong thread or fishing line, and 50 whole cayenne peppers. It's a good idea to wear disposable surgical gloves (available at drug stores) when working with the peppers, as they can burn. Never touch a pepper, then touch your eye with your hand. It will burn! Thread the needle and tie a loop at one end. Run the needle through the peppers just below the stem and slide to the end of the string. Repeat until you've reached the desired length. Remove the needle and tie a knot in the thread. Arrange peppers so they face in alternating directions. Hang vertically like the traditional southwestern "ristra." Fresh chilies will dry as they hang.

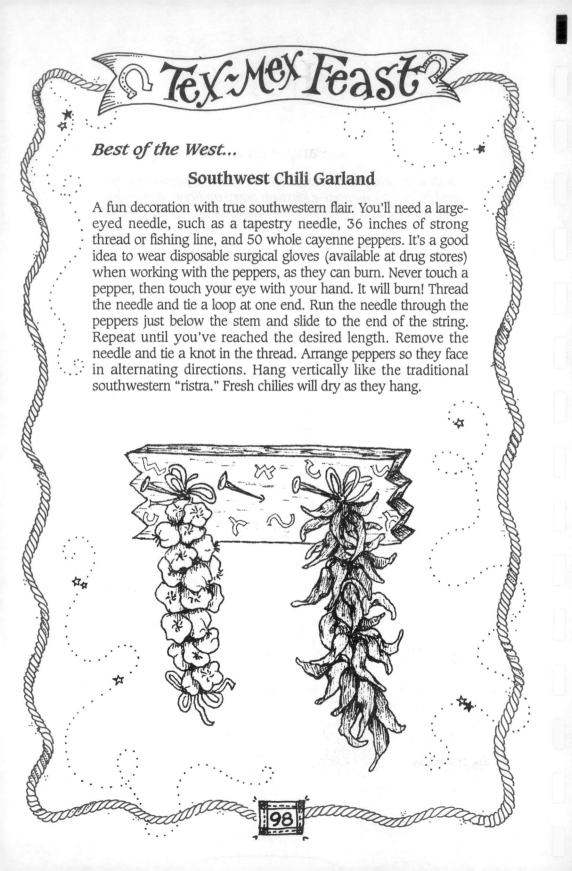

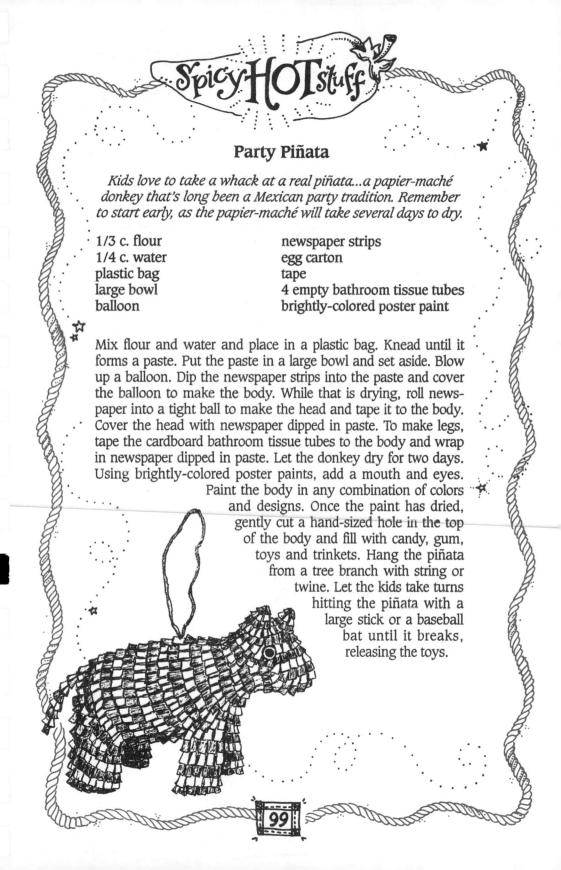

Party Piñata

Kids love to take a whack at a real piñata...a papier-maché donkey that's long been a Mexican party tradition. Remember to start early, as the papier-maché will take several days to dry.

1/3 c. flour	newspaper strips
1/4 c. water	egg carton
plastic bag	tape
large bowl	4 empty bathroom tissue tubes
balloon	brightly-colored poster paint

Mix flour and water and place in a plastic bag. Knead until it forms a paste. Put the paste in a large bowl and set aside. Blow up a balloon. Dip the newspaper strips into the paste and cover the balloon to make the body. While that is drying, roll newspaper into a tight ball to make the head and tape it to the body. Cover the head with newspaper dipped in paste. To make legs, tape the cardboard bathroom tissue tubes to the body and wrap in newspaper dipped in paste. Let the donkey dry for two days. Using brightly-colored poster paints, add a mouth and eyes. Paint the body in any combination of colors and designs. Once the paint has dried, gently cut a hand-sized hole in the top of the body and fill with candy, gum, toys and trinkets. Hang the piñata from a tree branch with string or twine. Let the kids take turns hitting the piñata with a large stick or a baseball bat until it breaks, releasing the toys.

Tex~Mex Feast

Weathered Clay Pot Planters

These planters are so easy, and look great potted with a variety of cactus plants, Mexican heather or herbs. Just rub the outside of new clay pots with buttermilk. Let them stand for three weeks in a shaded, damp area like a garage or basement. They'll look like they've been around since the pioneers settled the Old West!

Homemade Invitations

Make your own Tex-Mex party invitations. Purchase blank notes and envelopes, and cut them into simple western shapes like hats, boots, horses, cows or cacti. Use corks to decorate your invitations. Draw a pattern on the wide end of a cork...a star, heart, chili pepper or boot. Using a sharp knife, cut away the cork from the area outside the pattern, paring about 1/4 inch deep. Press the cork onto a stamp pad and press the design onto your invitations and envelopes. Use markers and gold glitter ("gold dust") to finish off your designs.

Picnic Fantasy

... lazy summer days

Salmon with Dill Sauce
Grilled Chicken Cobb Salad with Peppercorn Dressing
Sliced Tomatoes with Tarragon and Cream
Corn-Pecan Muffins
Orzo Salad with Garlic
Fresh Corn Salad
Rhubarb Crunch
Chocolate-Peanut Butter Cupcakes

There isn't time, there isn't time
To do the things I want to do –
With all the mountain tops to climb
And all the woods to wander through.
- Eleanor Farjeon

Picnic Fantasy

Salmon with Dill Sauce

This salmon tastes best when served warm or at room temperature.

2 to 3 lb. salmon fillet
1/2 c. soy sauce

1 t. black pepper,
   freshly cracked

Sauce:

1/2 c. heavy cream
1/4 c. water
1/4 c. olive oil

1/2 c. brown mustard
4 t. sugar
1/2 c. fresh dill, chopped

To prepare salmon, rinse and pat dry. Place skin-side down on foil-lined pan and rub with soy sauce. Season with pepper and broil for 12 to 15 minutes. To prepare dill sauce, whisk all ingredients together. To serve, pour sauce over individual servings of salmon.

Why use floppy paper plates for your picnic when plastic plates make eating so much easier? Easy to clean, earth-friendly and inexpensive.

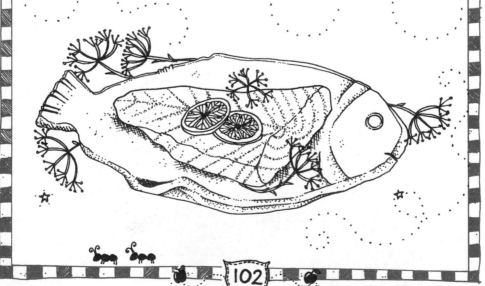

Grilled Chicken Cobb Salad with Peppercorn Dressing

A meal in itself!

3 or 4 chicken breasts, grilled and cubed
1/2 c. blue cheese, crumbled
1/2 c. tomatoes, diced
1/2 c. avocado, diced
1/2 c. bacon, cooked, drained and crumbled

1/2 c. hard-boiled eggs, diced
12 asparagus spears, blanched
6 c. lettuce (Romaine and red tip look beautiful)

Dressing:

1 1/2 c. light mayonnaise
1 1/2 c. sour cream
4 T. black pepper, freshly cracked
1 T. lemon juice

3/4 c. parmesan cheese, grated
salt to taste
1 c. water
1 T. fresh garlic, minced

Arrange chicken, blue cheese, tomatoes, avocado, bacon, eggs and asparagus on a platter lined with lettuce. In mixing bowl, whisk together dressing ingredients; mix well and spoon over salad.

Sliced Tomatoes with Tarragon and Cream

Red, ripe tomatoes, fresh from the garden, are a must.

1 T. fresh tarragon leaves, minced	1/4 t. coarse salt
1/4 c. heavy cream	4 ripe beefsteak
1/4 c. créme fraîche	tomatoes, sliced

Créme Fraîche:

1/2 c. whipping cream   1/2 c. sour cream

Whisk creams together and chill overnight.

In mixing bowl, whisk together tarragon, cream, créme fraîche and salt. Arrange tomatoes on serving platter and spoon on the cream sauce. Garnish with tarragon leaves, if desired and serve right away.

Corn-Pecan Muffins

1 1/2 c. cornmeal	1 1/2 c. milk
2 T. sugar	2 large eggs, beaten
1 1/4 c. flour	1/2 c. butter, melted
1 t. baking powder	1 c. pecans, finely chopped
1/4 t. salt	

Preheat oven to 400 degrees. Mix together cornmeal, sugar, flour, baking powder and salt. Stir in milk, eggs and butter; add pecans. Spoon batter into prepared muffin cups about 2/3 full. Bake muffins for about 25 minutes or until tester comes out clean.

Orzo Salad with Garlic

Orzo is very small, round pasta. You can also make this recipe with cooked brown rice...delicious!

1 1/4 c. orzo, cooked
2 cloves garlic, minced
3 T. fresh parsley, chopped
1/2 c. spinach leaves

6 T. olive oil
Garnish: red and yellow peppers, diced

Cook orzo according to package directions. In a small mixing bowl, whisk together garlic, parsley, spinach and oil. Add orzo while still warm and toss together. Refrigerate until chilled. Serve cold, topped with red and yellow peppers.

Garlic is easily minced when you smash the clove, still in the peel, with the side of the chopping blade. The peel will come right off, and the clove will be flat and easy to chop.

Rhubarb Crunch

Serve warm with a scoop of vanilla ice cream.

2 c. sugar
1 c. plus 2 T. flour
1/2 t. nutmeg
4 c. fresh rhubarb, cut into 1/2" lengths

2 T. butter
1/4 t. salt
1 t. baking powder
1 large egg, beaten

Preheat oven to 350 degrees. Sift together 1 cup sugar, 2 tablespoons flour and nutmeg and toss with rhubarb. Pour into an 8 or 9-inch pan and dot with butter. In another dish, sift together remaining sugar and flour with salt and baking powder and stir in beaten egg. The mixture will be crumbly. Sprinkle it over the rhubarb and shake the pan a little so the crumbs will settle down in the rhubarb. Bake about 40 minutes, until the crust is a delicate brown.

Auntie Rae's Rhubarb

When the voices of children
are heard on the green
And laughing is heard on
the hill,
My heart is at rest
within my breast
And everything else
is still.
- William Blake

Chocolate Peanut-Butter Cupcakes

A treat for any celebration. Make them extra special by dusting tops with powdered sugar using lace paper doilies or heart cut-outs.

Filling:

2 T. heavy cream
2 oz. semi-sweet chocolate, grated

2 t. sugar
1/4 c. smooth peanut butter

Cupcakes:

6 T. butter
6 oz. semi-sweet chocolate
2 large eggs
2/3 c. sugar

1 t. vanilla
3/4 c. flour, unsifted
1/4 t. baking soda
1/4 t. salt

To prepare filling, heat cream in small saucepan until boiling. In another bowl, pour cream over chocolate and sugar; stir until combined and chocolate melts. Add peanut butter and mix well. Refrigerate filling for 35 to 40 minutes until slightly firm. Preheat oven to 350 degrees. Prepare muffin tins by spraying with vegetable cooking spray. In double boiler over low heat, melt butter and chocolate. In mixing bowl, beat eggs until foamy. Add sugar and vanilla and beat until fluffy. Beating at low speed, add melted chocolate. Beat in flour, baking soda and salt and mix until just combined. Pour batter into muffin tins, filling almost 2/3 full. Roll rounded teaspoonfuls of filling and press one ball lightly into the center of each cupcake. Bake for 15 to 20 minutes.

Picnic Fantasy

Fresh fruit delights...

*What could be more delightful than fresh, ripe summer fruit?
We've gathered some quick, low-fat ideas for summer's
delicious bounty of berries, peaches, nectarines, melons
and cherries...refreshing endings for any picnic!*

Fruit Compote

Syrup:

1 c. water
1/2 c. sugar
3/4 c. fresh mint, chopped

1/4 c. bourbon
1 T. fresh lemon juice

Compote:

Most any summer fruit will do. Here's our recipe...

1/4 cantaloupe, seeded
1/4 honeydew, seeded
1/2 lb. sweet cherries, pitted
3 ripe peaches, thinly
   sliced

3 T. fresh mint, thinly
   sliced
fresh mint sprigs for
   garnish

To make syrup, combine water and sugar in a medium
saucepan over low heat until sugar dissolves. Add mint and boil
5 minutes over medium heat. Let cool completely. Strain into a
bowl, pressing firmly on the mint to extract flavor. Mix the
bourbon and the lemon juice into the syrup. Cover and refrigerate; can be made ahead of time. Scoop melons with a melon
baller. Combine all fruits, add syrup and toss. Refrigerate for 30
minutes. Spoon into pretty pedestal glasses and garnish with
mint sprigs.

*Here's a quick fruit salad dressing that's easy and delicious.
Beat one cup of softened vanilla ice cream with 3 tablespoons of
mayonnaise. Serve over your favorite fresh fruits.*

Raspberry Sorbet ☆

2 c. sugar
1 c. water
3 pints fresh raspberries

4 T. fresh lemon juice
fresh whole raspberries
    for garnish

Combine sugar and water in a small saucepan and simmer over medium heat for 5 minutes. Set aside to cool. Place raspberries, cooled syrup and lemon juice in a blender and purée. Strain and refrigerate. Freeze in an ice-cream machine, or in the freezer, stirring every so often until soft-frozen.

Melon Salsa

1 c. honeydew melon, cut
    into 1/4" cubes
1 c. cantaloupe, cut into 1/4"
    cubes
1 t. ginger, freshly grated

1/4 t. salt
3 T. scallions, minced
1 t. jalapeño pepper, seeded
    and minced
1 T. fresh lime juice

Toss all ingredients together in a medium bowl and refrigerate until cold. Delicious on grilled chicken sandwiches.

Fresh Peaches with Cinnamon Yogurt

1/2 c. plain yogurt
3 T. sugar

1 T. cinnamon
4 ripe peaches, peeled and
    sliced

Combine yogurt, sugar and cinnamon. Divide mixture evenly among four dessert cups. Arrange peach slices on top. Garnish with a sprinkle of cinnamon and fresh mint leaves.

Picnic Fantasy

Strawberries in a Nest

1 envelope unflavored gelatin
1/4 c. cold water
6 oz. cream cheese
3 T. sugar

1 c. milk
1/2 c. boiling water
6-oz. can frozen lemonade,
    thawed
1 quart strawberries, cleaned

Soften gelatin in cold water. Bring water to boiling to dissolve. In a separate bowl, mix cream cheese and sugar, gradually adding milk. Add gelatin to cream cheese and blend. Add lemonade and mix thoroughly. Pour into a 1-quart gelatin mold and chill until firm. Transfer mold onto a platter. Fill the center with ripe, red strawberries.

Cherry "Giggles"

A really fun finger food for kids of all ages! Make lots of different flavors.

2 pkgs. unflavored gelatin
1 1/2 c. cold water

1 c. hot water
6 oz. pkg. cherry gelatin

Dissolve unflavored gelatin in 1/2 cup of cold water and let stand 5 minutes. Measure 1 cup of hot water and add the package of cherry gelatin. Stir well so gelatin is dissolved. Add this to the unflavored gelatin and cold water mixture. Pour in remaining cold water and stir well. Pour into a 12"x7 1/2" dish and chill. When gelatin is solid, use cookie cutters to cut into fun shapes.

Coolest-Ever Family Campout

...hot off the grill

Chuck Wagon Dinner
Sloppy Joes
Pan-Fried Parsley Potatoes
Baked Bean Casserole
Hot Ham & Cheese Sandwiches
S'mores
Instant Gorp

Oh, give me a home where the buffalo roam,
Where the deer and the antelope play,
Where seldom is heard a discouraging word,
And the skies are not cloudy all day.
- Anonymous old cowboy song,
"Home on the Range"

Coolest ever Campout

Chuck Wagon Dinner

These terrific foil pack dinners can be prepared at home and packed in a cooler to toss on the coals at your first campfire. Or just prepare the vegetables; then everyone can easily make their own dinner.

heavy aluminum foil
1 lb. ground beef, shaped
   into 4 patties
1 medium onion, chopped
2 large potatoes, sliced

2 large carrots, sliced
1 small green pepper, diced
1 stalk celery, diced
16 oz. can tomatoes, drained
salt and pepper to taste

Lay 4 large sheets of foil on picnic table. Place one beef patty in center of each. Let each camper heap his own vegetables onto beef, placing tomatoes on top. Season each with salt and pepper. Bring ends of foil together and roll down tightly; fold ends to seal. Place on outer edge of coals, turning occasionally for even cooking; grill about 20 to 30 minutes. Be careful when you open your dinner...steaming hot vegetables inside!

Sloppy Joes

A quick, spicy sandwich loved by kids of all ages.
Cook in an iron skillet.

1/4 t. salt	1/2 t. black pepper
1 lb. lean ground beef	1/4 c. ketchup
1/4 c. onion, diced	1 t. yellow mustard
1 clove garlic, minced	1 t. Worcestershire sauce
1/2 t. celery salt	6 fresh, soft hamburger buns
2 t. chili powder	

Sprinkle salt on an iron skillet and heat over the campfire grill. Crumble hamburger into the skillet and cook and stir until it begins to turn brown. Add onion and garlic and cook until onion is limp. Add all remaining ingredients (except buns) and heat thoroughly. Spoon onto buns and serve.

Pan-Fried Parsley Potatoes

A real treat for breakfast!

1 1/2 t. fresh parsley, chopped	1 stick unsalted butter
3/4 t. dried thyme	4 to 5 potatoes, thinly
salt and freshly ground pepper,	sliced
to taste	

In a zipping plastic bag, shake together parsley, thyme, salt and pepper. In a heavy skillet, melt 2 tablespoons butter and remove from heat. Cover bottom of skillet with potato slices and dot with butter. Sprinkle on herbs and repeat layers. Cook potatoes over fire until golden and crispy on the bottom, flipping once, about 10 to 15 minutes on each side. Cut into squares and serve hot.

Baked Bean Casserole

Good energy and protein for hikers and campers.

1 lb. dried navy beans
8 ozs. bacon, cut into small pieces
1 c. onions, chopped
2 c. ketchup

6 T. maple syrup
6 T. molasses
1/4 c. Worcestershire
   sauce
salt and pepper, to taste

In a large pot of water, soak beans overnight. Rinse beans under cold water and place in heavy saucepan. Cover with water and bring to a boil. Reduce heat and simmer for one hour or until beans are tender. Drain and reserve liquid. In heavy skillet, fry bacon and onions until onions are transparent and bacon is slightly crisp. Add ketchup, syrup, molasses and Worcestershire sauce. Stir in drained beans, mixing well. Cover and let simmer over hot coals, stirring occasionally for 1 1/2 to 2 1/2 hours until flavors are blended and beans are tender. Season with salt and pepper. Add some of the reserved bean liquid occasionally to make a thick sauce.

The night will never stay,
The night will still go by,
Though with a million stars
You pin it to the sky;
Though you bind it with
the blowing wind,
And buckle it with the moon,
The night will slip away
Like sorrow or a tune.
- Eleanor Farjeon

Hot Ham & Cheese Sandwiches

Sandwich filling can be made ahead and kept in a cooler until ready to use.

2 c. baked ham, cubed
3/4 lb. mild Cheddar cheese, grated
1 large onion, chopped
20 ripe olives, chopped

3 or 4 green chili
   peppers, chopped
8 oz. can tomato juice
12 crusty hard rolls

Mix all ingredients (except rolls) in a bowl and keep cool until you're ready to make the sandwiches. Cut the top crust off the hard rolls and scoop out the inside, reserving bread crumbs for the birds. Fill rolls with the ham mixture. Replace top crust and wrap each sandwich individually in foil. Heat over campfire 10-15 minutes, turning every so often to heat evenly. Carefully unwrap and enjoy.

Baked Potatoes with Blue Cheese

The blue cheese topping makes them special!

4 large baking potatoes, scrubbed
1/4 c. blue cheese
1/2 c. sour cream

2 T. dry ranch salad
   dressing mix
1 green onion, chopped

Wrap potatoes in foil and poke several holes through foil and potato skin with a fork. Bake over coals for at least an hour or until tender. While baking, prepare topping by mixing together blue cheese, sour cream, salad dressing seasoning and onion. Split hot baked potatoes lengthwise and fluff with a fork. Spoon on topping and serve right away. Makes 4 servings.

Coolest ever Campout

S'mores

Most everyone remembers these favorites. S'mores have been around so long, they're sure to bring back special memories for the grownups, and create new ones for the kids.

pkg. of graham crackers
pure milk chocolate bars
   (quantities will vary
   depending on appetites)

large bag of marshmallows
long sticks for roasting
   marshmallows

Place at least two marshmallows on a stick and roast marshmallows over the campfire until golden and hot. (Or crisp and bubbly...your choice!) Place chocolate squares on one half of graham cracker and, using the other graham cracker, carefully remove marshmallows from stick and squish on top of chocolate. Wait a minute to allow marshmallow to cool and chocolate to melt (if you can wait that long). Serve with a smile.

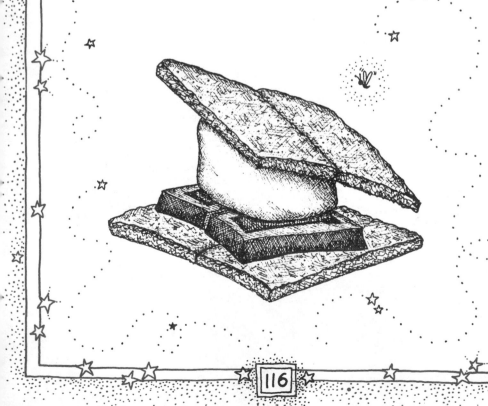

Instant Gorp

Prepare before your camping trip and spoon into sealed plastic bags. The perfect snack for hungry hikers!

2 c. raisins
2 c. peanuts

2 c. granola (plain or fruit)
2 c. chocolate chips

Mix all ingredients together and it's ready to go!

Spread peanut butter on a banana and coat with "gorp" for a delicious snack!

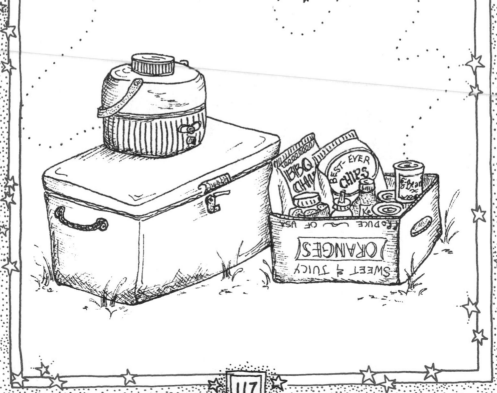

Coolest ever Campout

Fun outdoorsy ideas...

Campers' Mailbox

Here's a fun idea for a large group if you're camping for several days. Make a "mailbox" out of a gallon-sized plastic ice cream tub with a handle. Using a utility knife, cut a slit into the tub lid, wide and long enough to receive "mail." Paint and decorate the tub any way you'd like, with family members' names, initials, slogans and symbols. Hang the tub on a tree branch. The kids will enjoy sending secret messages. Be sure to pack pads of paper and pens for notes!

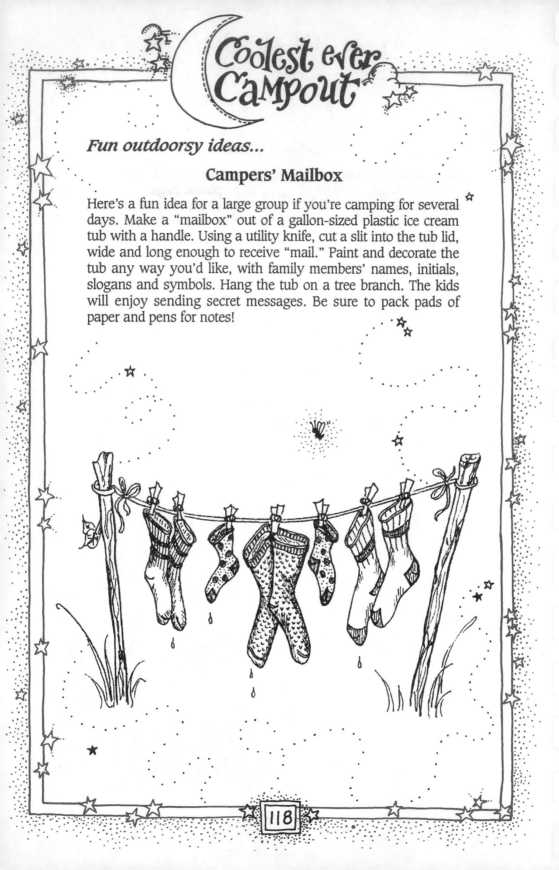

Terrarium

glass container (like a fishbowl)   natural soil
bits of charcoal   plastic bags
small pebbles   spade or large spoon

Making a terrarium is a good camping project for kids. First, be sure plant-collecting is allowed where you'll be camping...get permission if necessary. Pack a glass container to hold your terrarium...a large fishbowl or wide-mouthed mayonnaise jar will be perfect. Put a layer of charcoal on the bottom (plain charcoal briquettes will work very well). The charcoal will keep your terrarium from decaying. Next, put a layer of pebbles over the charcoal. The pebbles will help the water to drain away from the roots of the plants. The next layer is soil, which you can get from wherever the plants are growing. Collect tiny plants that grow near one another, because these are the ones that will do well in the terrarium. With a large spoon and some plastic bags, collect mosses, miniature ferns, myrtle, wintergreen and false lily of the valley. (You may want to look these plants up so you'll be able to recognize them.) Dig the plants as deeply and as gently as you can, keeping the roots intact. Plant as soon as possible. Water them and press them firmly into the soil. Put the moss in last to form a carpet. Add a few pretty stones to make a little woodland scene. Keep your terrarium in a spot where it will get some light, and water once a week with a spray bottle. The glass container will act as a greenhouse, keeping the plants moist and warm.

Braided Bird Wreath

Make a picnic for the birds...they'll flock to this summertime treat, and you'll enjoy watching the birds at your campground.

1 lb. frozen bread dough, thawed
1 egg
1/2 c. wild bird seed

Grease the outside of a 9-inch round cake pan and place on a greased cookie sheet. Roll out dough into a 30-inch rope. Using a sharp knife, cut the dough into thirds lengthwise and braid. Place braided dough around the outside of the cake pan and seal the edges by pinching them together. Cover with a clean dish towel and let rise 30 minutes, or until double in size. Bake in a preheated 375 degree oven for 20 minutes. While bread is baking, whisk egg in a small bowl. Remove bread from the oven, brush with egg, sprinkle with bird seed and bake 10 minutes longer. Remove from the pan and let set for 24 hours uncovered. Hang outside for the birds to enjoy!

Woodland Potpourri

Go on a gathering expedition for potpourri ingredients. Look for little pine cones and sprigs of pine, bayberries, wild roses, lavender and violet blossoms, wild mint and sage. (Be sure you're camping in a place where picking is allowed!) Anything that smells good will work. When you get home, you can add orange and apple slices, lemon peel, mace, cinnamon sticks and cloves. Spread your potpourri on a cookie sheet in a single layer and dry in the shade. When completely dry, mix the ingredients and put in jars with tight-fitting lids.

Campfire Tips

You don't have to be an expert to know how to build a campfire. For a wood fire:

Begin by clearing an area around the site. Gather some rocks to form a ring around the clearing, building up the sides to about 6 or 8 inches. Start with lighting "tinder," something that burns easily like small dry twigs, wood shavings or crumpled paper. (If you have some old candle stubs, place them in the center; this ensures your fire will catch.) Make a small pile of sticks stacked like a teepee loosely around the shavings or paper. Add larger sticks and then logs of hard wood as the fire matures. Keep feeding your fire every hour or so until you have deep, hot coals. To extinguish, smother the fire with "clean" dirt or sand (no leaves or sticks) and douse with water. Make sure coals are completely extinguished, and litter is gathered, before leaving your campsite.

Baking soda is an excellent fire extinguisher to keep on hand at your campsite.

Index

strawberry shortcake 🍓 barefoot in the grass · hot dogs on the grill · fireworks · red, white & blue · farmer's market · misty mornings · berry picking · lemonade · summer vacations · sandy beaches · dandelions · "school's out" · butterflies

Gooseberry Patch Originals

WELCOME HOME for the HOLIDAYS
your companion from September through December

to from harvest through Christmas... a treasury of holiday recipes, decorating tips, & traditions & easy-to-make gifts

Old-Fashioned Country Christmas

A holiday keepsake of recipes, traditions, homemade gifts, decorating ideas, & favorite childhood memories

OLD-FASHIONED COUNTRY COOKIES
hundreds of recipes, tips, & ideas

Old-Fashioned Country Cookies

Yummy recipes, tips, traditions, how-to's, and sweet memories... everything Cookies

OLD-FASHIONED COUNTRY CHRISTMAS
our all-time BEST SELLER!

GOOD FOR YOU!
recipes, fun ideas, heartwarming stories, good for body, mind, soul

For Bees & Me

A Bouquet of Garden-Fresh Recipes, Memories, Hints, Simple Pleasures, Herbal Beauty Potions, Backyard Entertainment & Easy-To-Make Gifts

FOR BEES & ME
garden-fresh recipes, backyard entertaining & gifts from the garden

Good For You!

A collection of good food, good fun, good stories for the body, mind & soul!

Gooseberry Patch Originals

Reserve your copies today!

Homespun Christmas

HOMESPUN CHRISTMAS
A heartwarming collection of Christmas recipes, tips, and ideas

Treasured family recipes, memories, homemade decorations, heartfelt gifts & holiday traditions

Celebrate Spring

A freshly gathered bouquet of tender recipes, brand new how-tos and tempting tips for the joyous days of springtime.

Collect the WHOLE Set!

Celebrate Summer

A star-spangled collection of luscious recipes, carefree tips and easy how-tos for long, lazy summer days.

Celebrate Autumn

A bushel of fresh-picked fall recipes, tips & how-tos for the festive season of friends & family.

Celebrate Winter

A warmhearted collection of recipes for joyful holidays, sparkling celebrations & cozy fireside feasts.

strawberry shortcake 🍓 barefoot in the grass

hot dogs on the grill 🌭 fireworks 🎆 red,white&blue 🚩 farmer's market

summer vacations ⭐ sandy beaches 🌾 dandelions 🌻 school's out 🦋 butterflies

lemonade 🍋 berry picking 🍓 misty mornings ☀️

GOOSEBERRY PATCH
P.O. Box 190, Dept. CELU
Delaware, OH 43015

A Country Store In Your Mailbox®

Please send me the following Gooseberry Patch books:

Book	Quantity	Price	Total
Old-Fashioned Country Christmas	————	$14.95	————
Welcome Home for the Holidays	————	$14.95	————
Old-Fashioned Country Cookies	————	$14.95	————
For Bees & Me	————	$17.95	————
Good For You!	————	$14.95	————
Homespun Christmas	————	$14.95	————
Celebrate Spring	————	$12.95	————
Celebrate Summer	————	$12.95	————
Celebrate Autumn	————	$12.95	————
Celebrate Winter	————	$12.95	————
		Merchandise Total	————
		Ohio Residents add 6 1/4%	————

Shipping & handling: Add $2.50 for each book. Call for special delivery prices.

Quantity discounts and special shipping prices available when purchasing   Total   ————
6 or more books. Call and ask! Wholesale inquiries invited.

Name: _____

Address: _____

City: _____ State: _____ Zip: _____

We accept checks, money orders, Visa or MasterCard (please include expiration date). Payable in U.S. funds only. Prices subject to change.

- -

GOOSEBERRY PATCH
P.O. Box 190, Dept. CELU
Delaware, OH 43015

A Country Store In Your Mailbox®

♡ How to Order ♡
For faster service on credit card orders,
call toll-free 1-800-85-GOOSE!
(1-800-854-6673)

Please send me the following Gooseberry Patch books:

Book	Quantity	Price	Total
Old-Fashioned Country Christmas	————	$14.95	————
Welcome Home for the Holidays	————	$14.95	————
Old-Fashioned Country Cookies	————	$14.95	————
For Bees & Me	————	$17.95	————
Good For You!	————	$14.95	————
Homespun Christmas	————	$14.95	————
Celebrate Spring	————	$12.95	————
Celebrate Summer	————	$12.95	————
Celebrate Autumn	————	$12.95	————
Celebrate Winter	————	$12.95	————
		Merchandise Total	————
		Ohio Residents add 6 1/4%	————

Shipping & handling: Add $2.50 for each book. Call for special delivery prices.

Quantity discounts and special shipping prices available when purchasing   Total   ————
6 or more books. Call and ask! Wholesale inquiries invited.

Name: _____

Address: _____

City: _____ State: _____ Zip: _____

We accept checks, money orders, Visa or MasterCard (please include expiration date). Payable in U.S. funds only. Prices subject to change.

strawberry shortcake 🍓 barefoot in the grass 🦶 hot dogs on the grill 🌭 fireworks 🎆 red, white & blue 🇺🇸 farmer's market 🍅 misty mornings 🫐 berry picking 🍊 lemonade ☀️ summer vacations ⭐ sandy beaches 🏖️ dandelions 🌼 school's out 🦋 butterflies